Halloween in the 1940s

Matt Philip

Published by Bright Minds Books, 2024.

While every precaution has been taken in the preparation of this book, the publisher assumes no responsibility for errors or omissions, or for damages resulting from the use of the information contained herein.

HALLOWEEN IN THE 1940S

First edition. September 22, 2024.

Copyright © 2024 Matt Philip.

ISBN: 979-8227187000

Written by Matt Philip.

Table of Contents

Description

Halloween in the 1940s explores the transformation of a beloved holiday during one of the most turbulent decades in American history.

From homemade costumes and wartime rationing to the post-war boom and the rise of commercialized celebrations, this book takes readers on a nostalgic journey through how Halloween was celebrated in small towns and big cities alike. Through 15 detailed chapters, it examines the roles of schools, churches, ghost stories, and trick-or-treating traditions in shaping the Halloween we know today.

Perfect for history buffs, nostalgia lovers, and Halloween enthusiasts, this book offers a fascinating glimpse into the past.

Dedication

To the children of the 1940s, whose creativity and resilience made Halloween magical despite the challenges of the era. And to the storytellers, parents, and teachers who kept the spirit of the holiday alive, inspiring future generations to celebrate with joy, imagination, and a sense of community.

This book is dedicated to those who transformed ordinary October nights into memories filled with laughter, mystery, and fun. Thank you for keeping the light of Halloween glowing brightly through difficult times, and for leaving behind a legacy of celebration that continues to inspire us today.

Preface

Halloween has always been a holiday filled with magic, mystery, and a touch of the supernatural, but its celebration in the 1940s held a special significance. As the world grappled with the challenges of war and recovery, Halloween provided a much-needed escape from reality, offering moments of joy and creativity in a time of hardship.

This book was inspired by the stories, traditions, and memories of those who grew up during this remarkable decade. It delves into the cultural and social dynamics that shaped Halloween celebrations, from the resourcefulness of wartime parties to the post-war boom in candy, costumes, and decorations.

I hope this book gives readers a glimpse into how Halloween evolved in the 1940s, reminding us of the enduring power of community, tradition, and imagination. Whether you are a Halloween enthusiast or simply curious about history, I invite you to explore the magic of this beloved holiday in a bygone era.

Chapter 1: The Cultural Landscape of the 1940s

The 1940s was a decade marked by significant upheaval and transformation. World War II dominated the first half of the decade, and the war's impact reached every facet of American life, including how holidays like Halloween were celebrated. The war effort demanded sacrifices from all citizens, from soldiers on the front lines to families on the home front. The economic and social landscape of the time was shaped by patriotism, rationing, and a focus on community. As Halloween approached each year, these factors heavily influenced how people observed the holiday.

Wartime Sacrifices and Rationing

The United States entered World War II in 1941, after the attack on Pearl Harbor, and by then, the war had already affected daily life across the globe. For Americans, rationing became a reality, and essential goods such as sugar, gasoline, rubber, and metals were tightly controlled by the government to ensure that enough resources were allocated for the war effort. These restrictions naturally affected celebrations, including Halloween.

Before the war, Halloween was already becoming a popular holiday, but the elaborate parties and festivities of the 1920s and 1930s were difficult to sustain in a time of shortages. Families could no longer afford extravagant decorations or costumes, and the availability of candy was limited due to sugar rationing. The impact of these constraints, however, did not erase the holiday spirit; rather, it fostered a sense of creativity and resourcefulness among Americans.

Homemade solutions became the norm, with many households crafting their own costumes from available materials. Simple, practical costumes made from old sheets, household linens, or other repurposed clothing became commonplace. The lack of commercial goods did not mean the end of Halloween; it simply changed the way people celebrated, with a focus on ingenuity rather than indulgence.

The Importance of Community

The war also heightened the sense of community and shared experience in America. In the 1940s, Halloween became an opportunity for neighborhoods to come together, often organizing group events that fostered solidarity and provided a brief respite from the anxieties of wartime. Many communities held Halloween parties at local schools, churches, or community centers to maintain the holiday's traditions and provide safe spaces for children to enjoy the festivities.

This sense of unity was also reflected in Halloween decorations. Instead of elaborate displays, people decorated their homes with items they already had on hand or created themselves. Homemade lanterns, carved pumpkins, and paper cutouts were common, as families prioritized creativity over consumerism. Despite the limitations, Halloween still brought a touch of lightheartedness to communities, providing a temporary escape from the grim realities of war.

Halloween also offered an opportunity to blend patriotism with festivity. Many decorations and costumes incorporated patriotic themes, with children dressing up as soldiers, sailors, and nurses. Red, white, and blue accents were often woven into the holiday décor. The blending of Halloween with patriotic pride served as a reminder of the country's unity and resilience during such a challenging time.

Entertainment and Popular Culture in the 1940s

The 1940s were also shaped by significant advancements in entertainment. As television was still in its infancy, radio and movies dominated American culture, offering people an escape from the stress of wartime. Halloween in the 1940s was often influenced by the media of the time, particularly radio dramas and Hollywood films that embraced spooky themes. Families would gather around the radio to listen to chilling Halloween specials, and the popularity of horror films soared during the decade.

Radio broadcasts like Orson Welles' *The War of the Worlds*, which aired in 1938, still resonated with listeners into the 1940s. Although this particular broadcast had caused panic when it was first aired due to its realistic portrayal of a Martian invasion, it helped solidify radio's power as a medium for Halloween entertainment. The idea of gathering around the radio for ghost stories or eerie dramas became a Halloween tradition in many households during this time.

Similarly, Hollywood contributed to the rise of Halloween-themed entertainment. The 1940s saw a surge in horror films, such as *The Wolf Man* (1941) and *Frankenstein Meets the Wolf Man* (1943). These films influenced the kinds of costumes and themes that emerged during Halloween celebrations. Children and adults alike would dress as classic monsters, and haunted house attractions often drew inspiration from the popular horror films of the time.

Patriotism and the War Effort

World War II deeply affected American consciousness, and Halloween was no exception. The holiday became a time for communities to come together not just in celebration, but also in support of the war effort. Throughout the war years, Halloween events often included activities designed to raise morale or support the troops. In some cases, Halloween parties were organized as fundraisers to purchase war bonds or gather supplies for soldiers overseas.

Children, in particular, were encouraged to engage in patriotic Halloween activities. Schools and community groups organized events where kids could participate in Halloween parades or carnivals that featured war-related themes. These events not only allowed children to enjoy the holiday but also reinforced the idea that everyone, including the youngest citizens, had a role to play in supporting the country during wartime.

Halloween during the war years was thus both a moment of escapism and a reminder of the collective responsibility that citizens bore. The spirit of the holiday remained intact, but its form had changed to reflect the times.

The Role of Family and Tradition

Despite the war and its challenges, Halloween remained a family-centered holiday in the 1940s. Parents took great care in making sure their children could still enjoy Halloween, even if it was on a smaller scale. Many families continued to carve pumpkins, make homemade costumes, and create their own traditions around the holiday, ensuring that the spirit of Halloween was passed on to the next generation.

In rural areas, where access to goods was often even more restricted, families relied heavily on local customs and traditions. These might include apple bobbing, telling ghost stories around the fire, or hosting small gatherings at the local schoolhouse or community center. In urban areas, families often took part in larger, city-organized events, such as parades and block parties, which also helped maintain the holiday's spirit.

As the decade wore on and the war ended in 1945, the cultural landscape began to shift. Families looked forward to a return to normalcy, and the post-war period would see a resurgence in consumerism, which would eventually bring back the more commercial aspects of Halloween. However, the years of the war left a lasting impression on how the holiday was celebrated, infusing it with a sense of resourcefulness, community, and shared responsibility.

Chapter 2: Halloween Costumes in the 1940s

Halloween costumes have always been central to the holiday's festivities, allowing people to explore their creativity and embrace the spirit of fun, fear, or fantasy. In the 1940s, costume-making faced a unique set of challenges due to World War II, but it remained an integral part of the celebration. The creativity of homemade costumes, coupled with cultural influences like movies and radio, defined the look of Halloween in the 1940s. From rationed materials to patriotic themes, the costumes of this era reveal a lot about the social and cultural mindset of the time.

Homemade Creativity: Making Do with Less

One of the most distinctive aspects of Halloween costumes during the 1940s was the widespread reliance on homemade designs. World War II had placed many restrictions on the types of materials that could be purchased for civilian use. Fabrics like cotton and wool, as well as rubber and metals used for costume accessories, were diverted for military purposes. As a result, families turned to household items to craft Halloween costumes, embracing the necessity of "making do" with what they had.

Children's costumes often consisted of items readily available in the home. Old bed sheets were frequently transformed into ghost costumes, with eyeholes cut out to create a simple, spooky look. Other costumes were assembled from repurposed clothing—parents might modify a worn-out dress to transform their child into a witch or a princess, or cut up an old shirt to make a cowboy outfit. This DIY approach to costumes not only reflected wartime austerity but also fostered a sense of resourcefulness and ingenuity.

Parents played a crucial role in helping their children design and create costumes. Sewing skills became valuable, as many costumes were hand-stitched. It wasn't uncommon for mothers to spend weeks leading up to Halloween creating costumes from scratch, using patterns from magazines or even sharing ideas with neighbors to come up with clever designs. The effort put into these homemade costumes gave Halloween a personal, family-oriented touch that distinguished it from the commercialized holiday it would later become.

Patriotic Themes: Halloween in the Time of War

With the war effort dominating public consciousness, it was natural for patriotic themes to seep into Halloween costumes. During the early 1940s, many costumes reflected the national mood of support for the troops. Children frequently dressed up as soldiers, sailors, and nurses, reflecting the heroes they admired on the battlefield. These costumes often echoed the military uniforms seen in newsreels and on posters, with many children proudly donning makeshift versions of the khaki, olive green, or navy blue uniforms worn by the armed forces.

Parents encouraged these patriotic costumes, as they aligned with the broader goal of keeping morale high on the home front. It wasn't just children, either—adults, too, would sometimes dress in patriotic costumes, especially if they were attending community Halloween parties or morale-boosting events. Women might dress as Rosie the Riveter, the iconic symbol of working women during the war, while men might fashion themselves as wartime pilots or factory workers.

The red, white, and blue color palette became a common feature in Halloween costumes, particularly after the United States' entry into the war in 1941. Even costumes that weren't directly tied to military themes—such as clowns, animals, or classic Halloween characters—would sometimes incorporate patriotic colors as a subtle nod to the war effort.

Influence of Movies and Radio

Despite the challenges posed by rationing, popular culture still had a significant influence on Halloween costumes in the 1940s. Movies and radio were the dominant forms of entertainment, and both mediums helped shape costume trends.

The 1940s was a golden age for monster movies, and characters from these films frequently appeared as Halloween costumes. Universal Pictures, the studio behind many iconic horror films, dominated the genre with releases like *The Wolf Man* (1941), *Frankenstein Meets the Wolf Man* (1943), and *The Ghost of Frankenstein* (1942). These films brought creatures like werewolves, vampires, and the Frankenstein monster into the popular imagination, making them prime candidates for Halloween costumes.

Children and adults alike would recreate these monstrous figures using whatever materials they could find. A pair of rubber gloves might serve as Frankenstein's hands, while a bit of makeup could turn a child into a werewolf or vampire. Face paint, which wasn't rationed, became an important part of many costumes, allowing for the transformation into a variety of ghoulish figures. Hair was often styled or dyed using temporary means to complete the look—Frankenstein's bride, with her shock of white-streaked hair, became a popular choice for older children or teenagers looking to emulate the gothic glamour of the silver screen.

Radio also contributed to the Halloween costume landscape. Although listeners couldn't see the characters on their favorite radio shows, they could imagine them. Popular radio programs like *The Shadow* and *The Green Hornet* inspired costumes based on the descriptions of these crime-fighting characters. The auditory nature of radio storytelling encouraged listeners to envision their own interpretations, leading to a wide range of costume designs inspired by radio dramas.

Radio provided another layer of imagination, especially for children. Without visual prompts, they were free to create costumes based on their interpretation of the voices and sounds they heard. This creative freedom allowed for some of the most original and inventive costumes of the era.

Classic Halloween Figures: Witches, Ghosts, and Skeletons

Of course, no discussion of Halloween costumes in the 1940s would be complete without mentioning the enduring appeal of classic

Halloween figures. Despite the war and the challenges of finding materials, costumes like witches, ghosts, and skeletons remained perennial favorites.

These classic figures were particularly popular because they required little in the way of specialized materials. A witch costume, for example, could be easily assembled from an old black dress, paired with a pointed hat made from construction paper or cardboard. A skeleton costume might be created using black clothing and white paint to depict bones on the fabric.

Ghosts, as mentioned earlier, were perhaps the simplest of all Halloween costumes, often made from bed sheets with holes cut for the eyes. These timeless characters allowed families to participate in Halloween traditions without needing to spend much money or time.

Commercialization and the Rise of Store-Bought Costumes

The latter half of the decade saw the gradual reintroduction of store-bought costumes, as manufacturers resumed production once the war ended in 1945. Companies like Ben Cooper and Collegeville, which had produced Halloween costumes in the 1930s, began to re-enter the market, offering affordable, ready-made costumes for children.

These early mass-produced costumes were often based on popular characters from movies, radio, and comic strips. By the late 1940s, it was possible to purchase costumes of characters like *Superman* or *Captain Marvel,* signaling the beginning of a trend that would explode in the 1950s and beyond. However, even as store-bought options became available, many families still preferred the tradition of homemade costumes, which carried a sense of personalization and family involvement.

Conclusion: Costumes as a Reflection of the Times

Halloween costumes in the 1940s were a reflection of the broader social and cultural dynamics of the decade. The resourcefulness required by wartime rationing, combined with the influence of popular culture and the strong sense of patriotism, shaped the way people dressed up for

Halloween. The war limited the availability of materials and also inspired creativity, leading to costumes that were both simple and imaginative.

As the decade progressed, Halloween costumes began to shift toward the more commercialized versions that would dominate in later years. But in the 1940s, costumes remained a family affair, shaped by the realities of the time and the enduring desire to celebrate, even in the face of hardship.

Chapter 3: Trick-or-Treating Traditions

Trick-or-treating is now a hallmark of Halloween celebrations, with millions of children across the United States donning costumes and going door-to-door in search of candy. However, in the 1940s, trick-or-treating as we know it was still in its formative stages. The practice had begun to take hold in the late 1930s but wasn't as widespread or as commercialized as it became in later decades. For families during the 1940s, trick-or-treating was shaped by a variety of factors, from wartime rationing to local community customs, and the tradition evolved throughout the decade in response to broader societal changes.

The Early Days of Trick-or-Treating

Trick-or-treating had its roots in ancient customs of going door-to-door during festivals, asking for food or money in exchange for prayers or performances. By the early 20th century, these practices had evolved into the more playful version of trick-or-treating that we recognize today. By the late 1930s, the phrase "trick or treat" was becoming a regular part of the Halloween vocabulary in certain regions of the United States, although it was far from the universal tradition it is now.

In the 1940s, trick-or-treating began to spread, but it wasn't yet a fully developed tradition in every community. Some areas embraced it early on, while others were slower to adopt the practice. Trick-or-treating was largely seen as a children's activity, with kids going door-to-door in their neighborhoods, often accompanied by parents or older siblings. It was a fun way for children to engage with the community, but there were limits on how far it could be taken, especially during the war years.

The Impact of World War II on Trick-or-Treating

World War II had a significant impact on trick-or-treating traditions in the 1940s. The war affected virtually every aspect of life, from what people ate to how they celebrated holidays. Rationing, a key feature of life during the war, directly influenced Halloween celebrations, and trick-or-treating was no exception.

One of the most important items rationed during the war was sugar, which made it difficult for families to give out candy to trick-or-treaters. Instead of the store-bought candy that became the norm in later years, families in the 1940s often gave out homemade treats or small gifts. Homemade cookies, popcorn balls, apples, and even small cakes were common items handed out on Halloween night. Sometimes, children might receive small tokens, such as buttons or crayons, as treats instead of food.

Candy was scarce, but communities found ways to keep the spirit of trick-or-treating alive. Children were still encouraged to dress up and go door-to-door, but they might collect a variety of different "treats" based on what families could spare. This practice fostered a sense of community and shared experience, as families participated in the holiday despite the restrictions imposed by the war.

Safety and Supervision

Trick-or-treating in the 1940s was generally a more supervised activity than it is today. Older children might go out in groups on their own, while younger children were typically accompanied by parents or older siblings. This supervision was partly due to safety concerns, as communities were more close-knit, and neighbors looked out for each other's children.

In many cases, trick-or-treating was organized as part of a broader community event. Neighborhoods would sometimes coordinate so that certain homes were designated as stops for children, creating a planned route that ensured kids were safe and neighbors were prepared to participate. In smaller towns and rural areas, trick-or-treating might involve visiting only a handful of homes, often of friends and family, rather than roaming through entire neighborhoods.

Safety was also emphasized in terms of the homemade treats given out. Since many of the treats were prepared at home, parents were generally more trusting of what their children received from neighbors. This stands in contrast to the later decades when concerns about tainted candy would cause parents to be more cautious about what their children ate.

The "Trick" in Trick-or-Treating

Today's trick-or-treating is generally focused on the "treat" aspect. However, in the 1940s, there was still a notable emphasis on the "trick." The idea behind trick-or-treating was that children would receive a treat, but if no treat was provided, they might play a harmless trick on the homeowner. In some communities, this playful mischief was a significant part of the Halloween experience.

The tricks played by children in the 1940s were often lighthearted and usually harmless, but they reflected a mischievous side of Halloween that is less emphasized today. Some of the pranks included soaping windows, knocking over garbage cans, or covering trees in toilet paper. In some cases, children might move lawn furniture or playfully tease their neighbors. These tricks were rarely mean-spirited, and most homeowners took them in stride, recognizing them as part of the holiday's fun.

Communities sometimes tried to rein in the trickster aspect of Halloween by organizing alternative activities. Schools, churches, and community centers would host Halloween parties or carnivals to keep children entertained and prevent them from engaging in too much mischief. These organized events often included games, treats, and costume contests, allowing kids to enjoy Halloween in a more controlled setting.

The Transition Toward More Treats and Less Tricks

As the decade wore on and the war ended in 1945, trick-or-treating began to shift away from tricks and more toward treats. The post-war period saw an increase in consumerism, and by the late 1940s, candy manufacturers began to recognize Halloween as a prime opportunity to market their products. With sugar rationing lifted, store-bought candy became more accessible, and households began to hand out small, individually wrapped candies to trick-or-treaters.

The commercialization of Halloween, which began in the late 1940s, would only grow in the following decades, but it laid the foundation for the trick-or-treating we recognize today. Candy companies such as Hershey's and Mars started to advertise their products specifically for Halloween, and by the 1950s, pre-packaged candy had largely replaced homemade treats as the preferred handout.

Regional Variations in Trick-or-Treating

In the 1940s, trick-or-treating traditions varied depending on where you lived. In some rural areas, the practice of going door-to-door for treats was less common, as houses were spread out, making it difficult for children to visit multiple homes. Instead, children in these areas might participate in community gatherings, such as Halloween parties at schoolhouses, or in small parades organized by the local church or community center.

In urban areas, trick-or-treating was more widespread, with children often able to visit many homes in a single evening. City neighborhoods were more densely packed, and this made trick-or-treating a popular activity for children who could cover several blocks in a short period. Even in urban areas, though, trick-or-treating was often limited to familiar neighborhoods, as parents preferred their children to stick close to home.

Different regions also had their own customs and names for the activity. In some parts of the Midwest, children didn't say "trick or treat" when they knocked on doors; instead, they might recite a rhyme or sing a short song. In other areas, trick-or-treating was part of larger Halloween traditions that included parades, costume contests, and games.

Trick-or-Treating as a Growing Tradition

By the end of the 1940s, trick-or-treating had become a more widespread and accepted part of Halloween celebrations, though it was still evolving. Communities continued to shape and refine the practice, and it wouldn't be until the 1950s that trick-or-treating would fully take off as a national tradition. The end of wartime rationing and the rise of consumerism allowed the practice to flourish, setting the stage for the candy-filled Halloween nights that would define the holiday in the second half of the 20th century.

Despite its limitations during the 1940s, trick-or-treating provided a sense of normalcy and fun for children growing up during a tumultuous decade. Whether receiving homemade cookies or pulling playful pranks on their neighbors, children in the 1940s experienced Halloween in a way that reflected the challenges and spirit of the times.

Chapter 4: Wartime Halloween Celebrations

The 1940s were a decade deeply marked by World War II, which dominated American life from 1941 until the war's conclusion in 1945. During these years, nearly every aspect of daily living, including holidays and traditions, was influenced by the war effort. Halloween was no exception. Wartime Halloween celebrations in the 1940s took on a unique character, blending traditional festivities with themes of patriotism, community support, and a sense of shared sacrifice. Wartime restrictions like rationing and curfews shaped the way Halloween was celebrated. However, communities across the country still found ways to enjoy the holiday, often using it as a brief respite from the difficulties of life during wartime.

Rationing and Resourcefulness

One of the most significant challenges to celebrating Halloween during the war years was the widespread rationing of key goods. The U.S. government instituted strict rationing measures to ensure that resources were available for the war effort, which affected nearly every household. Items such as sugar, rubber, gasoline, and certain fabrics were tightly controlled, and these shortages impacted the way Americans celebrated holidays, including Halloween.

Sugar rationing, in particular, played a significant role in altering Halloween traditions. Prior to the war, Halloween was a time for indulgence in sweets and candies, but with sugar rationed beginning in 1942, families had to get creative. Instead of handing out candy, many people gave trick-or-treaters homemade treats, like cookies sweetened with honey or molasses, popcorn balls, or fruit. Apples were a common Halloween treat, as they were both readily available and inexpensive.

Halloween costumes also reflected the scarcity of materials during the war. Store-bought costumes were rare during the early 1940s due to fabric shortages, so families turned to homemade options. Using old clothes, household linens, or repurposing other items, families crafted costumes that were simple but inventive. Old bed sheets became ghost costumes, while old uniforms could be transformed into outfits for cowboys or soldiers. Sewing and mending skills became essential for parents creating costumes for their children.

Even decorations were often homemade, as mass-produced decorations were in short supply. Families used materials like construction paper, cardboard, and household items to create jack-o'-lanterns, paper cutouts of witches and ghosts, and other traditional Halloween symbols. The DIY aspect of Halloween during the war emphasized a return to simplicity, with families often making decorations and costumes together as a way to celebrate.

Patriotic Themes in Halloween

As the country was fully immersed in the war effort, patriotism became an important part of public life, and this extended to holidays like Halloween. Celebrations were often infused with patriotic themes as a way to boost morale and encourage support for the troops overseas. Halloween offered an opportunity to combine traditional spooky fun with the serious message of national solidarity and resilience.

Patriotic Halloween costumes became a common sight during the war. Children would dress up as soldiers, sailors, nurses, and other war-related figures, reflecting the admiration they had for the men and women serving in the military. Many children had fathers, brothers, or other relatives fighting overseas, and dressing up as a member of the armed forces became a way to show support for their loved ones. Red, white, and blue color schemes were popular for both costumes and decorations, as families sought to blend their Halloween festivities with a sense of national pride.

In addition to costumes, Halloween events and parades often took on a patriotic flair. Community events, such as school or church-sponsored Halloween parties, would sometimes include war bond drives or other activities aimed at raising money for the war effort. These events served a dual purpose: they allowed children and families to enjoy Halloween while also contributing to the country's wartime needs. Halloween parades might feature floats or decorations celebrating American military victories, and patriotic songs were sometimes sung in addition to the usual Halloween-themed music.

Community Gatherings and Morale-Boosting Events

During the war, Halloween took on added significance as a time for community gathering and morale-building. The war had introduced a level of uncertainty and anxiety into daily life, and holidays like Halloween provided a welcome opportunity for people to come together, have fun, and temporarily escape the stresses of wartime. Local communities, schools, and churches often organized Halloween parties and events as a way to foster a sense of unity and lift spirits during difficult times.

In many towns and cities, Halloween parties were hosted by local schools or community centers, offering safe, organized spaces for children to celebrate. These events typically featured costume contests, games, and themed decorations. Bobbing for apples, pinning the tail on the donkey, and sack races were common party games that didn't require expensive materials, making them popular choices for wartime Halloween parties. In some cases, the parties were also used to teach children about the importance of the war effort, with activities like writing letters to soldiers or collecting scrap materials to support the war effort.

Halloween carnivals and parades were also a popular way for communities to celebrate the holiday during the war. These events, often organized by local civic groups or schools, allowed people to come together and show off their homemade costumes and decorations. Some towns held Halloween-themed talent shows or musical performances, which provided entertainment for both children and adults. The focus of these events was on fostering a sense of togetherness and maintaining a semblance of normalcy during a time when so much was uncertain.

Halloween for Soldiers Overseas

Families on the home front were celebrating Halloween in creative and resourceful ways when soldiers stationed overseas were also marking the holiday, albeit in very different circumstances. Despite being far from home and often engaged in difficult and dangerous combat, American soldiers still found ways to celebrate Halloween. In many military camps and bases, soldiers would organize Halloween parties or simple get-togethers to enjoy a brief break from the realities of war.

In some cases, soldiers received Halloween care packages from loved ones back home, filled with letters, treats, and decorations. These packages helped soldiers maintain a connection to home and provided a morale boost during a time when holidays could feel particularly lonely. Homemade cookies, dried fruit, and small gifts were commonly sent, as many of the popular Halloween candies were unavailable due to rationing.

On military bases, soldiers might decorate their barracks with makeshift Halloween decorations or organize costume contests using whatever materials they had on hand. These celebrations were often modest compared to the parties happening back home, but they served as a reminder of the normal life soldiers were fighting to protect. Halloween celebrations overseas also allowed soldiers to bond with each other, offering moments of levity and camaraderie amidst the challenges of wartime.

Halloween Radio Programs and Movies

Entertainment was an essential part of keeping spirits high during the war, and radio played a key role in Halloween celebrations during the 1940s. Families would gather around the radio to listen to Halloween-themed broadcasts, which often featured spooky stories or special holiday programming. Some of the most popular radio programs of the time, such as *Suspense* or *Lights Out*, aired Halloween episodes that captivated audiences with their eerie tales.

The war didn't stop Hollywood from producing horror films, either. Many of the major studios were focused on war-related films. Classic monster movies like *The Wolf Man* (1941) and *Frankenstein Meets the Wolf Man* (1943) were still popular during the war years. These films provided a form of escapism for audiences, allowing them to immerse themselves in fantasy worlds filled with monsters and ghouls, far removed from the grim realities of war.

For soldiers and civilians alike, Halloween movies and radio programs were a way to maintain a sense of tradition and enjoyment during the holiday. They offered a brief reprieve from the pressures of wartime life, allowing people to indulge in the thrills and chills of Halloween while still honoring the broader war effort.

The Lasting Impact of Wartime Halloweens

As the war came to a close in 1945, Halloween celebrations began to return to some semblance of normalcy, but the experience of wartime Halloween left a lasting impact. The resourcefulness and creativity that defined Halloween during the war years became a point of pride for many families. The post-war period would see a return to mass-produced costumes, decorations, and candy. Homemade traditions that flourished during the war persisted in many communities for years to come.

Wartime Halloween celebrations also reinforced the importance of community and togetherness, values that would continue to shape the holiday in the years following the war. For those who lived through the 1940s, Halloween during the war was not just about spooky costumes or trick-or-treating, but also about resilience, patriotism, and maintaining a sense of joy even in the most challenging of times.

Chapter 5: Post-War Halloween Boom

The end of World War II in 1945 brought significant changes to American society. The post-war years saw the beginning of a new era, marked by economic prosperity, increased consumerism, and a renewed focus on leisure and entertainment. As soldiers returned home, families reunited, and the economy transitioned from wartime production to a booming consumer market, holidays like Halloween began to evolve in significant ways. The late 1940s ushered in a period of renewed enthusiasm for Halloween, as access to consumer goods, candy, costumes, and decorations became more readily available. This chapter explores the post-war Halloween boom and how it shaped the way the holiday was celebrated in the latter half of the 1940s.

The Economic Boom and Consumerism

The end of the war brought about a period of unprecedented economic growth in the United States. The manufacturing sector, which had been focused on producing goods for the military, transitioned to producing consumer goods for the American public. This shift helped fuel a post-war economic boom, with increased wages, greater job security, and a rise in disposable income for many families. As a result, Americans had more money to spend on leisure activities, including holiday celebrations.

For Halloween, this economic prosperity meant a resurgence in the availability of consumer goods that had been restricted or unavailable during the war. Candy, which had been in short supply due to sugar rationing, once again filled store shelves, allowing families to indulge in the treats that had been scarce for years. Candy manufacturers, eager to capitalize on the growing post-war consumer market, began marketing their products specifically for Halloween. Companies like Hershey's, Mars, and Brach's advertised candy as an essential part of the holiday, encouraging families to buy pre-packaged sweets for trick-or-treaters.

This shift toward commercial candy transformed trick-or-treating in the post-war years. During the war, children had often received homemade treats like cookies, popcorn balls, and fruit, but by the late 1940s, pre-packaged candy had become the standard. Candy bars, gumdrops, caramels, and lollipops were among the most popular items handed out to trick-or-treaters, as the emphasis on convenience and abundance became a hallmark of post-war Halloween celebrations.

The Rise of Store-Bought Costumes and Decorations

Alongside the resurgence of candy came the return of store-bought Halloween costumes and decorations. During the war, fabric shortages had made it difficult for manufacturers to produce mass quantities of costumes, forcing families to rely on homemade creations. However, as the post-war economy boomed, costume manufacturers like Ben Cooper and Collegeville resumed production, offering affordable, ready-made costumes for children.

These costumes, often made of lightweight materials like rayon or plastic, were simple yet effective. Popular characters from movies, radio shows, and comic books were frequently featured in costume designs, reflecting the growing influence of mass media on Halloween. Children could dress up as characters like *Superman, Captain Marvel,* or even *Frankenstein's monster*—a far cry from the homemade ghosts and witches of the wartime years. The availability of these costumes made Halloween more accessible to families, as parents no longer had to spend time sewing or crafting costumes by hand.

Decorations, too, became more commercialized in the post-war years. Homemade decorations had been the norm during the war. However, families in the late 1940s could once again purchase mass-produced Halloween items, such as paper skeletons, black cats, and cardboard pumpkins. Department stores and dime stores stocked Halloween décor alongside costumes and candy, creating a one-stop shopping experience for families eager to celebrate the holiday. This commercialization of Halloween marked the beginning of the holiday's transformation into the consumer-driven event it would become in later decades.

The Influence of Mass Media

The late 1940s saw a surge in the influence of mass media, particularly film and radio, on Halloween celebrations. Movies, in particular, played a key role in shaping Halloween trends. The post-war years coincided with the golden age of horror films, and classic monster movies became a major part of Halloween culture. Universal Pictures, which had already established itself as the leader in horror films during the 1930s and early 1940s, continued to produce popular films featuring iconic characters like Dracula, Frankenstein, and the Wolf Man.

These films fueled the imaginations of children and adults alike, inspiring Halloween costumes, party themes, and decorations. Frankenstein's monster, with his green skin and towering frame, became a popular choice for Halloween costumes, as did the caped figure of Dracula and the furry, fearsome Wolf Man. For older children and teenagers, horror films became a favorite part of Halloween festivities, with many movie theaters hosting Halloween screenings of classic monster films.

Radio, still the dominant form of entertainment in many households, also contributed to the Halloween experience. Popular radio programs like *Suspense* and *The Shadow* aired special Halloween episodes, drawing listeners in with eerie tales of ghosts, ghouls, and supernatural happenings. Families would gather around the radio on Halloween night to listen to these spooky broadcasts, adding an extra layer of excitement and fear to the holiday.

The rise of television, though still in its early stages in the late 1940s, also began to influence Halloween celebrations. By the end of the decade, more American households were acquiring television sets, and TV programming began to shape holiday traditions in new ways. Halloween-themed TV shows and cartoons would soon become a staple of the holiday, but it was radio and film that dominated Halloween entertainment in the immediate post-war years.

Community Events and Halloween Parties

Community events and Halloween parties remained a central part of the holiday. Schools, churches, and civic organizations continued to host Halloween parties for children and families, offering a safe and structured way to celebrate the holiday. These events often featured costume contests, games, and prizes, allowing children to show off their store-bought or homemade costumes.

Community Halloween events also became an opportunity for fundraising and civic engagement. Many towns organized Halloween parades, where children could march in costume, and local businesses would sponsor floats or contribute prizes for costume contests. These parades, often followed by parties or carnivals, helped strengthen the sense of community in post-war America, as families came together to celebrate in the aftermath of the war.

In some areas, Halloween parties were also organized as a way to control or minimize the mischief that had traditionally been a part of the holiday. Vandalism and pranks, such as soaping windows or tipping over trash cans, had been common in earlier decades, but community leaders sought to channel children's energy into more constructive activities. Organized Halloween events provided a fun alternative to mischief, while also reinforcing the holiday's focus on community and family.

A Return to Normalcy

For many Americans, the late 1940s represented a return to normalcy after the disruptions of the war. Halloween, like other holidays, took on new significance as families sought to re-establish traditions that had been set aside during the war years. With soldiers returning home, families growing, and a booming economy, Halloween became a time for celebration and enjoyment. The abundance of consumer goods, combined with the influence of mass media and the growing commercialization of the holiday, made Halloween a much-anticipated event for children and adults alike.

The renewed emphasis on family and community in the post-war years also influenced how Halloween was celebrated. Families were eager to create lasting memories for their children, and Halloween provided the perfect opportunity for bonding, creativity, and fun. Whether it was trick-or-treating through the neighborhood, attending a community parade, or listening to a spooky radio broadcast together, Halloween in the late 1940s was a joyful occasion that reflected the optimism and prosperity of the era.

The Foundations of Modern Halloween

The post-war Halloween boom of the late 1940s laid the foundation for the holiday's modern form. The commercialization of Halloween, with its focus on store-bought costumes, candy, and decorations, was just beginning, but it would only grow in the coming decades. Trick-or-treating became a more established tradition, while mass media—through films, radio, and eventually television—played an increasingly important role in shaping Halloween culture.

Halloween was becoming a major holiday in its own right, one that was eagerly anticipated by children and embraced by adults. The innovations and trends of the late 1940s would continue to shape Halloween for generations to come, making it the widely celebrated, fun-filled event it is today.

Chapter 6: Halloween Parties and Social Gatherings

Halloween parties and social gatherings became an essential part of the holiday during the 1940s, reflecting the values of community, family, and fun that were central to post-war American life. They offered a more structured and communal way to celebrate, particularly during the early years of the decade when wartime restrictions affected how the holiday was observed. These gatherings ranged from intimate family events to large community celebrations, often including games, food, costumes, and storytelling.

The Importance of Community

During the 1940s, especially in the early years of World War II, community involvement became a critical aspect of Halloween celebrations. With many resources directed toward the war effort, families and neighborhoods relied heavily on each other for support and companionship. Halloween parties became a way to lift spirits, provide entertainment, and maintain a sense of normalcy during uncertain times. Schools, churches, and civic organizations often hosted these events, offering a space for children and adults alike to come together and celebrate.

The focus on community during Halloween parties was also a reflection of the broader social climate of the 1940s. With many fathers, brothers, and sons serving overseas, families on the home front leaned on each other for support. Halloween parties allowed neighbors to gather, share homemade treats, and enjoy each other's company, providing a brief respite from the worries of the war. These events were often modest but filled with fun and creativity, making the most of limited resources.

School and Church-Sponsored Parties

One of the most common venues for Halloween parties in the 1940s was the local school or church. These institutions played a significant role in organizing holiday events, particularly for children. School Halloween parties were often held during the day, with classrooms decorated with paper pumpkins, black cats, and ghosts. Children would come to school dressed in their homemade or store-bought costumes, and the day would be filled with festive activities.

At school-sponsored Halloween parties, games were a major part of the entertainment. Classic games like bobbing for apples, pin the tail on the donkey (often with a Halloween twist, such as pinning the hat on the witch), and sack races were popular choices. These games required minimal materials, which made them ideal for wartime celebrations when resources were scarce. In some schools, teachers would read spooky stories to their students or lead them in singing Halloween songs, further adding to the festive atmosphere.

Churches also played an important role in Halloween celebrations. Many churches organized community-wide Halloween events, offering a safe and family-friendly environment for the holiday. These gatherings often featured costume contests, where children could show off their creative outfits and compete for small prizes. In addition to games and contests, church-sponsored Halloween events frequently included potluck dinners, where families contributed homemade dishes to share with the community. These potlucks became a way for families to bond and celebrate together, even during difficult times.

House Parties: Family and Friends

Many families preferred to host their own Halloween parties at home, inviting friends and neighbors for an evening of spooky fun. These house parties were typically smaller and more intimate but no less enjoyable. Families would decorate their homes with homemade decorations, often made by the children, and prepare a variety of treats for their guests.

In the early 1940s, wartime rationing meant that families had to be creative when it came to party food. Instead of store-bought candy, homemade snacks like popcorn balls, caramel apples, and cookies sweetened with honey or molasses were common. These treats, while simple, were eagerly anticipated by children and adults alike. In some cases, families would hold pumpkin-carving contests, with everyone trying to create the scariest or most creative jack-o'-lantern.

Storytelling was also a key element of many house parties. Parents or older siblings would gather the children around and tell ghost stories or recount local legends, adding a sense of mystery and excitement to the evening. These stories often featured themes of haunted houses, ghosts, and witches, drawing from both traditional folklore and popular culture. For families living in rural areas, where trick-or-treating might not have been as widespread, these Halloween parties provided a way to engage in the holiday's spirit without leaving the house.

Traditional Games and Activities

Halloween parties in the 1940s were filled with traditional games and activities that had been passed down through generations. These games were often simple but brought a lot of joy to the participants. Bobbing for apples was one of the most popular activities at both school and home Halloween parties. This game, which involved trying to grab apples floating in a tub of water using only your mouth, had its roots in old harvest festivals and was a staple of Halloween gatherings.

Another popular activity was fortune-telling, which added a mystical element to the evening's entertainment. Children and adults alike would try to predict their future through various means, such as reading tea leaves, cracking eggs into water to interpret the shapes, or using mirrors to supposedly glimpse their future spouse. These fortune-telling games were all done in the spirit of fun, though they were often taken quite seriously by the children involved.

Costume contests were also a common feature of Halloween parties in the 1940s. These contests allowed both children and adults to show off their creativity, with prizes awarded for the scariest, funniest, or most original costume. Some families opted for store-bought costumes in the post-war years, while many still made their own, incorporating homemade elements or using whatever materials were on hand. Winning a prize at a Halloween costume contest was a source of great pride, especially for children who had spent weeks planning and crafting their outfits.

Themed Parties and Decorations

By the late 1940s, themed Halloween parties were becoming increasingly popular, particularly among older children and teenagers. These parties often had specific themes, such as a "haunted house" or "witches' ball," and guests were encouraged to dress in costumes that matched the theme. The decorations at these parties were often more elaborate, with homemade haunted house setups, dim lighting, and spooky sound effects creating a truly immersive experience.

For teenagers, Halloween parties provided an opportunity to socialize and enjoy a sense of independence. These gatherings were often held in basements, garages, or barns, where teenagers could dance to the popular music of the time and participate in more grown-up activities, like murder mystery games or horror movie screenings. These parties allowed teenagers to celebrate Halloween in a way that was different from the more innocent and child-focused activities of earlier years.

Halloween parties also reinforced the values of community and togetherness that were so important in the 1940s. Whether at a school, church, or home, Halloween parties brought people together, creating lasting memories and helping to build strong bonds within neighborhoods and families.

Post-War Changes in Halloween Parties

As the war ended and the United States entered the post-war period, Halloween parties became more extravagant. With the lifting of rationing and the return of consumer goods, families were able to purchase more candy, decorations, and costumes for their parties. Store-bought decorations and costumes, which had been scarce during the war, became widely available in the late 1940s, making it easier for families to throw festive Halloween parties with all the trimmings.

The post-war period also saw the rise of organized entertainment at Halloween parties. In addition to traditional games and activities, some parties featured hired entertainers, such as magicians or fortune-tellers, to add a sense of spectacle to the event. These larger, more elaborate parties reflected the growing commercialization of Halloween and the increasing emphasis on consumer culture in the post-war years.

Families continued to gather for homemade treats, costume contests, and spooky stories, blending old traditions with new trends. These Halloween parties laid the foundation for the more elaborate and commercial celebrations that would come in the following decades, but they remained rooted in the values of togetherness and creativity that had always been at the heart of Halloween.

Chapter 7: Halloween Decorations

Halloween decorations are one of the most recognizable aspects of the holiday, setting the stage for spooky fun and transforming homes into eerie, haunted spaces. In the 1940s, Halloween decorations took on a special significance, blending old traditions with new, homemade designs shaped by wartime rationing and a growing sense of community. From simple jack-o'-lanterns carved at the kitchen table to more elaborate homemade decorations designed to stretch limited resources, Halloween in the 1940s showcased the creativity and spirit of families and communities working within the confines of their time.

Homemade Decorations and Wartime Creativity

Wartime shortages during the early 1940s greatly affected how people decorated their homes for Halloween. Materials such as rubber, metal, and even certain types of paper were being rationed or redirected for the war effort, limiting access to the kinds of mass-produced decorations that would become common in the later decades. As a result, families had to rely on their ingenuity to create festive Halloween environments with what they had at home.

One of the most common and iconic homemade decorations of the time was the jack-o'-lantern. Pumpkins were widely available and inexpensive, making them a favorite choice for families looking to add a spooky touch to their porches or windowsills. Carving a jack-o'-lantern became a family activity, with parents and children gathering around the kitchen table to cut out eerie faces, often using simple tools like kitchen knives or spoons. The flickering light from a candle or a small lantern placed inside the pumpkin created a haunting glow, serving as a welcoming (or warning) signal to trick-or-treaters.

Homemade paper decorations were also a staple of 1940s Halloween. Families would cut out silhouettes of black cats, witches, and ghosts from construction paper or cardboard, hanging them in windows or pinning them to the walls. These paper cutouts were inexpensive to make and could be crafted from materials that were often already available at home. Many children took part in creating these decorations, using scissors and glue to fashion spooky shapes that would be proudly displayed around the house.

In addition to paper cutouts, families often crafted makeshift Halloween decorations using household items. For example, old clothes could be stuffed with straw or newspaper to create scarecrows or dummy figures that could be posed in front yards or on porches. Empty tin cans, old rags, and other everyday items could be repurposed into spooky decorations with a little imagination. These homemade creations reflected the resourcefulness of families during the war years and helped to maintain the holiday spirit despite the limitations of rationing.

Patriotic Halloween Décor

The 1940s were heavily influenced by World War II, and this national focus on patriotism naturally extended to holiday celebrations, including Halloween. Many Halloween decorations during the war years blended traditional spooky themes with patriotic symbols as a way to show support for the troops overseas. Families might combine the colors of Halloween—black and orange—with red, white, and blue elements, incorporating flags or patriotic bunting into their décor.

In some communities, Halloween parades or parties featured decorations that honored the military. Homes would display patriotic banners alongside jack-o'-lanterns, and school Halloween parties might be decorated with pictures of soldiers, planes, and American flags, giving the holiday a distinctly wartime flavor. This blend of Halloween and patriotism allowed families to celebrate the holiday while also contributing to the broader national effort to support the troops and boost morale on the home front.

Post-War Changes in Decorations

As the war ended in 1945, American life began to shift toward peacetime prosperity, and Halloween decorations reflected this transition. With the easing of rationing and the return of mass-produced goods, families once again had access to store-bought decorations. By the late 1940s, paper companies like Beistle began producing affordable Halloween decorations, which became a popular addition to homes, schools, and community centers.

These commercially produced decorations often featured familiar Halloween imagery, such as witches, bats, skeletons, and pumpkins, and were printed in bright colors on lightweight paper or cardboard. These decorations were easy to hang and could be reused from year to year, making them a convenient choice for families looking to create a festive atmosphere. Mass-produced paper garlands, cutouts, and window clings became widely available, allowing families to decorate more extensively and with less effort than in the wartime years.

The post-war years saw a mix of homemade and store-bought decorations, with families incorporating both into their celebrations. This combination allowed for greater creativity and personalization, as families could choose which elements to purchase and which to craft themselves.

The Role of Schools and Community Centers

Schools and community centers were important venues for Halloween celebrations in the 1940s, and decorating these spaces became a central part of the holiday. Teachers and students would often work together to create festive environments for Halloween parties, using a mix of homemade and store-bought decorations. Construction paper chains, painted pumpkins, and tissue-paper ghosts were common classroom projects, with students taking pride in decorating their classrooms for the holiday.

In some communities, local businesses or civic organizations sponsored Halloween events, decorating public spaces like parks, town squares, or community halls. These larger-scale decorations often included banners, scarecrows, and even haunted house setups, where local volunteers would transform buildings or outdoor areas into spooky attractions. These community-driven events helped strengthen neighborhood bonds and provided safe, organized spaces for children to celebrate Halloween.

Lighting and Atmosphere

Lighting played a crucial role in setting the mood for Halloween in the 1940s. In many homes, simple candles or lanterns were used to create an eerie, flickering effect, particularly when placed inside jack-o'-lanterns or paper lanterns. In some cases, families would use colored light bulbs—typically red or green—to cast a spooky glow on their front porches or living rooms.

For those who could afford it, electric Halloween lights became more popular in the post-war years. String lights featuring small, pumpkin-shaped bulbs or lights shaped like bats or skulls could be hung along windows or porches, adding a more elaborate touch to outdoor decorations. Electric lights were still relatively new in the late 1940s. They hinted at the growing commercialization of Halloween and the increasing emphasis on creating eye-catching, festive displays.

Halloween Yard Displays

Yard displays were a popular way for families to get into the Halloween spirit in the 1940s, especially in the post-war years. Some families had simple front yard decorations, such as a carved pumpkin or a homemade scarecrow. Others went to greater lengths to transform their yards into spooky spectacles. These displays often included figures made from straw, old clothes, and other materials, representing witches, ghosts, or skeletons.

In rural areas, hay bales, cornstalks, and pumpkins were frequently used to create a harvest-themed Halloween display. These decorations celebrated both the spooky aspects of Halloween and the traditional autumn harvest, blending the two themes in a way that felt natural and appropriate for the season.

For children, these yard displays added an element of excitement to trick-or-treating. Going door-to-door in a neighborhood where homes were decorated with spooky figures, glowing pumpkins, and eerie lighting made the experience feel magical and immersive. Children would often compete to see who could spot the scariest or most creative decorations, turning the simple act of trick-or-treating into an adventure.

The Transition to More Commercial Decorations

By the end of the 1940s, the commercialization of Halloween was well underway, with companies producing more elaborate decorations each year. Cardboard cutouts, plastic figures, and electric lights became more common, making it easier for families to create festive Halloween displays with minimal effort. The increasing availability of store-bought items allowed families to expand their decorating options and create more elaborate displays.

This transition reflected broader societal changes in the post-war era, as American families began to embrace consumer culture and the convenience of store-bought goods. Halloween decorations, once limited by wartime shortages, became a reflection of this newfound prosperity, with families eager to celebrate the holiday in bigger and more elaborate ways.

Conclusion: The Evolution of Halloween Decorations

Halloween decorations in the 1940s reflected the broader societal shifts of the time, from the resourcefulness required during wartime to the increasing consumerism of the post-war years. Families in the early part of the decade relied heavily on homemade decorations, using whatever materials were available to create spooky environments. By the end of the decade, however, the rise of mass-produced decorations allowed for more elaborate and convenient displays, signaling the beginning of Halloween's transformation into the commercial holiday we know today.

Whether made by hand or purchased in a store, Halloween decorations in the 1940s played a crucial role in creating the festive, spooky atmosphere that defined the holiday. These decorations brought families and communities together, allowing them to celebrate the season with creativity, tradition, and fun.

Chapter 8: Halloween and the Movies

Halloween and the movies have long shared a connection, with the film industry playing a significant role in shaping the themes, costumes, and atmosphere of the holiday. In the 1940s, Halloween celebrations were influenced heavily by Hollywood, particularly in the realm of horror films and monster movies. As the country navigated the challenges of World War II and the economic recovery that followed, movies offered an escape for Americans and a source of inspiration for Halloween costumes and parties. This chapter explores how the movies of the 1940s influenced Halloween traditions, from iconic horror films to the rise of cinematic-themed Halloween celebrations.

The Golden Age of Horror Movies

The 1940s were a golden age for horror films, with many of the most iconic monsters and creatures making their mark on the big screen. Universal Pictures, in particular, dominated the genre during this era, creating a series of films that would come to define horror for generations. Monsters such as Frankenstein, Dracula, the Wolf Man, and the Mummy became household names, with these characters leaving an indelible mark on Halloween celebrations.

During the 1940s, Universal Pictures continued to produce sequels and crossovers featuring its classic monsters, further embedding these figures in American popular culture. Films like *The Wolf Man* (1941), *Frankenstein Meets the Wolf Man* (1943), and *The Ghost of Frankenstein* (1942) captivated audiences, blending horror with thrilling drama. These films not only entertained but also provided an escape from the grim realities of war, offering viewers a chance to lose themselves in a world of gothic horror and fantasy.

For Halloween, these iconic monsters became a major source of inspiration for costumes and decorations. Children dressed up as Frankenstein's monster, Dracula, and the Wolf Man, often using homemade materials to recreate the looks they had seen on the silver screen. Face paint and masks were popular ways to bring these characters to life, and homemade costumes often featured torn clothing, fake blood, and creative makeup to evoke the horror and mystery of these beloved monsters.

Horror movies also inspired the atmosphere at Halloween parties. Some families and community groups would create haunted house setups based on the settings of these films, complete with flickering lights, eerie music, and cobweb-covered rooms. Guests might be greeted by a Frankenstein's monster lookalike at the door, or enter a room styled like Dracula's gothic castle. These horror movie-themed parties allowed fans of the films to experience the thrills and chills of their favorite on-screen monsters in real life.

Horror Icons: Frankenstein, Dracula, and The Wolf Man

Among the many monsters that graced the silver screen in the 1940s, three stood out as Halloween favorites: Frankenstein's monster, Dracula, and the Wolf Man. These characters, popularized by Universal's horror films, became staples of Halloween costumes and decorations throughout the decade.

Frankenstein's monster, first brought to life by Boris Karloff in the 1931 film *Frankenstein*, remained a popular Halloween figure in the 1940s, especially with the release of *The Ghost of Frankenstein* (1942) and *Frankenstein Meets the Wolf Man* (1943). Children and adults alike dressed as the towering creature, using painted cardboard to mimic his square head and dark clothing to replicate his iconic look. Homemade versions of the monster often featured stitched-up faces, bolts attached to the neck, and green face paint to complete the transformation.

Dracula, portrayed by Bela Lugosi in the 1931 film, continued to be a prominent Halloween figure in the 1940s. With his slicked-back hair, black cape, and hypnotic stare, Dracula embodied the mysterious and aristocratic vampire that audiences loved. For Halloween, children and adults would don fake fangs, slick their hair back, and wear long, flowing black capes to emulate the infamous Count. Dracula-themed Halloween parties might feature candlelit rooms and gothic décor, with eerie organ music setting the tone for a spooky night.

The Wolf Man, a relatively new addition to the horror genre, became an instant hit when *The Wolf Man* premiered in 1941, starring Lon Chaney Jr. The film introduced audiences to the tragic story of Lawrence Talbot, a man cursed to transform into a werewolf with each full moon. The Wolf Man's hairy, ferocious look quickly made him a Halloween favorite, with children creating costumes using fur from old coats or blankets to mimic the creature's appearance. Face paint and homemade masks were often used to capture the werewolf's terrifying snout and fangs, making the Wolf Man one of the most memorable Halloween monsters of the decade.

The Role of Movie Theaters in Halloween Celebrations

Movie theaters played a key role in Halloween celebrations during the 1940s. As Halloween approached, theaters across the country often hosted special screenings of horror films, giving audiences the chance to experience their favorite monsters on the big screen. These screenings, which sometimes included double features or late-night showings, were a popular attraction for both children and adults, especially as Halloween night offered a perfect excuse for a spooky movie marathon.

In some towns and cities, theaters would go all out for Halloween, decorating their lobbies and auditoriums to match the horror films they were showing. Theaters might be draped in cobwebs, with skeletons, bats, and other spooky figures positioned throughout the space. Employees might even dress as characters from the films being screened, adding to the immersive experience for moviegoers.

In addition to horror films, movie theaters also showed Halloween-themed cartoons and short films, particularly for younger audiences. Characters like Mickey Mouse, Bugs Bunny, and other beloved cartoon figures appeared in Halloween specials, offering a lighter, more family-friendly form of Halloween entertainment. These cartoons were often shown alongside horror films, making for a varied and fun-filled Halloween outing at the theater.

The Impact of Radio on Halloween Entertainment

Movies played a major role in Halloween celebrations, but radio was also an important medium for delivering spooky thrills. In the 1940s, radio was still the dominant form of home entertainment, and families would gather around their radios on Halloween night to listen to special broadcasts of spooky stories and thrilling mysteries.

One of the most famous radio programs of the time was *Suspense*, which often aired Halloween-themed episodes that featured chilling tales of the supernatural. Another popular show, *Lights Out*, specialized in eerie, spine-tingling stories that kept listeners on the edge of their seats. For families tuning in on Halloween night, these radio dramas provided the perfect accompaniment to the holiday, setting a creepy atmosphere as ghost stories filled the airwaves.

Perhaps the most famous Halloween radio broadcast of all time occurred just before the 1940s began, in 1938, with Orson Welles' infamous adaptation of H.G. Wells' *The War of the Worlds*. Though this broadcast happened before the 1940s, its impact continued to be felt throughout the decade. The realistic nature of the broadcast, which led many listeners to believe that an actual Martian invasion was underway, became a part of Halloween folklore. In the years that followed, many radio programs took inspiration from this broadcast, offering listeners similarly immersive and frightening Halloween experiences.

Horror Movie-Themed Halloween Parties

The influence of movies extended beyond costumes and decorations into the realm of Halloween parties, where cinematic themes became a popular choice for hosts looking to entertain their guests. Horror movie-themed Halloween parties were a common sight in the late 1940s, with hosts transforming their homes into settings inspired by the silver screen.

At these parties, guests might be greeted by a host dressed as Count Dracula or the Wolf Man, and the house itself might be decorated to resemble a haunted castle or an eerie forest. Homemade props, such as cardboard coffins, flickering lights, and cobweb-covered furniture, helped create the illusion of stepping into a horror movie. In some cases, partygoers would act out scenes from their favorite films or participate in murder mystery games that echoed the plotlines of classic horror stories.

Movies also provided inspiration for Halloween games and activities. A popular party game in the 1940s involved guests trying to identify movie monsters based on descriptions or silhouettes, while others might compete in costume contests, with prizes awarded for the best movie monster look-alike. These cinematic-themed parties allowed fans of horror films to bring their favorite movies to life, blending the thrills of the big screen with the fun of Halloween.

The Legacy of 1940s Horror Movies on Halloween

The horror films of the 1940s left an enduring legacy on Halloween traditions. Characters like Frankenstein, Dracula, and the Wolf Man became synonymous with the holiday, their monstrous visages appearing on everything from costumes to decorations. The connection between Halloween and horror movies, which solidified in the 1940s, would only grow stronger in the decades to come, with films continuing to play a central role in Halloween celebrations.

The 1940s marked the beginning of the film industry's strong influence on Halloween. It also set the stage for future developments. In the years that followed, television and more advanced special effects would push Halloween movie celebrations to new heights, but the foundation laid by the classic monster movies of the 1940s would remain a beloved part of the holiday.

Chapter 9: Radio Shows and Halloween-Themed Entertainment

In the 1940s, radio was the dominant form of entertainment in most American homes. Families gathered around their radios to listen to news, music, and drama, often making it the focal point of their evenings. Halloween was a particularly exciting time for radio programming, with a variety of spooky and eerie shows designed to thrill and entertain listeners. These broadcasts became an essential part of Halloween celebrations during the decade, shaping how the holiday was experienced and remembered by those who tuned in. From spine-chilling horror stories to playful Halloween-themed comedies, radio brought Halloween to life in ways that would influence generations to come.

The Golden Age of Radio and Its Role in American Life

Before television became a fixture in American households, radio was the go-to medium for entertainment and information. By the 1940s, millions of families owned radios, and it was common for people to spend their evenings gathered around the radio to listen to their favorite shows. Radio programming was incredibly diverse, offering something for everyone: comedy, drama, variety shows, and news broadcasts. During the war years, radio also played an important role in keeping Americans connected to world events, with regular news bulletins about the progress of the war.

As a medium that relied on sound and imagination, radio had a unique ability to engage listeners. The lack of visual imagery meant that listeners had to visualize the scenes and characters in their minds, making radio an especially effective medium for Halloween-themed entertainment. Whether it was a chilling ghost story or a suspenseful thriller, radio dramas invited listeners to immerse themselves in the eerie atmospheres and spine-tingling tales that became so closely associated with Halloween.

Spooky Radio Dramas: Thrills and Chills

One of the most popular genres of radio programming during the 1940s was the suspense thriller. These shows, which often featured tales of murder, mystery, and the supernatural, were perfect for Halloween. Radio dramas such as *Suspense* and *Lights Out* became synonymous with Halloween thrills, offering listeners the chance to be scared from the comfort of their own homes.

Suspense was a long-running radio drama that aired from 1942 to 1962, becoming one of the most famous and beloved programs of the era. Known for its high-quality writing and production, *Suspense* specialized in tales that kept listeners on the edge of their seats. Many episodes featured ghostly apparitions, haunted houses, or mysterious disappearances, all of which made the show a favorite for Halloween. Episodes often featured well-known Hollywood stars of the time, lending an air of sophistication and credibility to the production. On Halloween, *Suspense* would air special episodes designed to terrify listeners, with some stories featuring unexpected twists and supernatural elements.

Another iconic show of the era was *Lights Out*, created by Wyllis Cooper and later directed by Arch Oboler. *Lights Out* was one of the earliest radio horror programs and was famous for its graphic and often gruesome stories. Unlike many radio shows of the time, which kept violence and gore offstage, *Lights Out* embraced the horror genre with gusto, featuring episodes that were designed to shock and scare. Episodes such as "The Dark" and "Revolt of the Worms" became legendary for their ability to terrify audiences. The show aired late at night, adding to the sense of fear and suspense, and Halloween episodes of *Lights Out* were some of the most eagerly anticipated broadcasts of the season.

These radio dramas were highly effective at creating a mood of suspense and dread, relying on sound effects like creaking doors, eerie footsteps, and ghostly wails to heighten the tension. Listeners' imaginations did the rest, conjuring up terrifying images to match the sounds they were hearing. For many people in the 1940s, Halloween wasn't complete without tuning in to hear a spooky story on the radio.

The Legacy of Orson Welles' *The War of the Worlds*

Although it aired in 1938, Orson Welles' infamous radio adaptation of H.G. Wells' *The War of the Worlds* continued to influence Halloween radio programming well into the 1940s. The broadcast, which famously caused panic among listeners who believed that Martians were invading the Earth, became a part of radio folklore. It wasn't intended as a Halloween program. However, the timing of the broadcast—October 30th, the night before Halloween—ensured that it would forever be associated with the holiday.

The impact of *The War of the Worlds* extended far beyond its initial broadcast. In the years that followed, radio stations often aired the program again on Halloween, giving new audiences the chance to experience the suspense and fear that had gripped listeners in 1938. The broadcast also inspired other radio shows to push the boundaries of what could be achieved with sound and storytelling, encouraging a new generation of writers and directors to experiment with thrilling, immersive narratives.

For Halloween in the 1940s, the legacy of *The War of the Worlds* helped solidify the idea that radio could be a powerful tool for creating fear and excitement. Even though television would later become the dominant medium, the influence of radio on Halloween traditions would endure, with the broadcast serving as a reminder of the power of sound to evoke emotions and spark the imagination.

Lighter Fare: Halloween-Themed Comedies and Variety Shows

Horror and suspense were the dominant genres for Halloween radio programming. Not all Halloween-themed broadcasts were designed to scare. Many popular comedy and variety shows of the time embraced the holiday as an opportunity for humor and lighthearted entertainment. Shows like *Fibber McGee and Molly*, *The Jack Benny Program*, and *The*

Great Gildersleeve often featured special Halloween episodes that focused on the fun and playful aspects of the holiday.

On *Fibber McGee and Molly*, a popular radio comedy that followed the antics of a Midwestern couple, Halloween episodes typically involved the characters getting into some kind of humorous trouble. In one memorable episode, Fibber McGee decides to play a prank on his neighbors by dressing up as a ghost, only to have the plan backfire in a series of comedic mishaps. The show's Halloween episodes were light and fun, offering listeners a break from the more serious or frightening programming that was popular at the time.

The Jack Benny Program, another beloved radio comedy, often embraced Halloween as an opportunity for clever jokes and character-driven humor. Jack Benny, known for his stinginess and self-deprecating wit, would often find himself in absurd situations involving trick-or-treaters, Halloween parties, or haunted houses. The show's witty dialogue and playful tone made it a favorite for families who wanted to celebrate Halloween without the scares.

Variety shows also got into the Halloween spirit, with musical performances, skits, and special guest stars adding to the festive atmosphere. These shows often included spooky sound effects, like howling wolves and cackling witches, but the overall tone was more playful than frightening. For listeners who preferred laughter to screams, these Halloween-themed variety shows were a welcome alternative to the more intense horror programming.

Halloween Stories for Children

In addition to adult-targeted horror shows and comedies, radio also offered Halloween-themed programming for children. Shows like *The Lone Ranger* and *Superman*, which were already popular with young listeners, often featured special Halloween episodes that blended adventure with spooky themes. These episodes might involve the heroes encountering haunted houses, solving ghostly mysteries, or outsmarting villains who used Halloween as cover for their crimes.

For younger children, educational and children's shows sometimes featured Halloween stories or songs. These programs aimed to introduce children to the holiday's traditions, such as trick-or-treating and pumpkin carving, while keeping the tone light and fun. Parents often encouraged their children to listen to these radio programs as part of their Halloween festivities, creating a sense of shared experience and excitement.

The Power of Sound in Halloween Radio

One of the reasons radio was so effective at creating a spooky Halloween atmosphere was its use of sound effects. Since radio relied entirely on sound to tell its stories, producers became experts at using noises to evoke fear, suspense, or laughter. Halloween radio dramas often featured creaking doors, howling winds, eerie footsteps, and ghostly voices, all of which worked together to create an immersive auditory experience.

Music also played a key role in setting the mood for Halloween radio shows. Shows like *Suspense* and *Lights Out* used haunting musical scores to heighten the tension and build anticipation, while comedies and variety shows incorporated light, festive tunes to match the holiday spirit. For listeners, these soundscapes were crucial to the Halloween experience, helping to transport them into the worlds of haunted houses, graveyards, and spooky forests.

The Legacy of Halloween Radio Shows

The radio shows of the 1940s left a lasting impact on how Halloween was celebrated and experienced. Long after radio's golden age had passed, the memories of tuning in to a spooky story on Halloween night remained vivid for those who grew up in the 1940s. Even as television and film became more dominant forms of entertainment, radio retained a special place in Halloween traditions, with classic episodes being re-aired on Halloween or remembered fondly by older generations.

Radio's ability to engage listeners' imaginations and evoke fear through sound alone was a testament to the power of storytelling, and its influence on Halloween would continue for decades to come.

48

Chapter 10: Halloween for Children in the 1940s

Halloween in the 1940s was a magical time for children, despite the limitations imposed by World War II and the societal challenges that came with it. The excitement of costumes, games, and treats created lasting memories for young Americans growing up during this decade. Halloween had not yet fully transformed into the commercial extravaganza we know today. The holiday was already well on its way to becoming a favorite for children across the country. This chapter explores how children celebrated Halloween in the 1940s, focusing on the traditions, costumes, games, and treats that made the holiday so special for young revelers.

Homemade Costumes: Creativity and Resourcefulness

For many children in the 1940s, homemade costumes were the highlight of Halloween. Unlike today, when store-bought costumes dominate, most families in the 1940s made their children's Halloween costumes at home. This was especially true during the war years when fabric and materials were rationed, and store-bought goods were harder to come by. Parents and children worked together to design costumes from old clothes, household items, and basic craft supplies, turning everyday materials into something magical.

Children often dressed as traditional Halloween characters like witches, ghosts, and skeletons, which were easy to create from simple materials. A ghost costume could be made from an old bed sheet with eyeholes cut out, while a witch's hat could be crafted from cardboard and black paint. Other children dressed as animals, clowns, or even soldiers, inspired by the patriotic mood of the time. The process of making a costume was often a family affair, with parents, siblings, and even neighbors offering ideas and helping with sewing or painting.

Despite the limitations of wartime rationing, children in the 1940s relished the chance to show off their costumes at school parties, community events, and while trick-or-treating. The creativity involved in making these costumes made them all the more special, as each one was unique and personal.

School Halloween Parties: A Day of Fun

Schools were central to children's Halloween celebrations during the 1940s. In the weeks leading up to Halloween, classrooms were often transformed with decorations like paper pumpkins, witches, and black cats. Teachers would lead students in crafting their own Halloween decorations, with children eagerly cutting out paper ghosts and drawing jack-o'-lantern faces to hang on classroom walls.

On Halloween day, many schools held parties or special activities for the students. Children would come to school dressed in their costumes, parading through the halls to show off their creative outfits to their classmates and teachers. Costume contests were common, with prizes awarded for the scariest, funniest, or most original costumes. These contests provided an opportunity for children to take pride in their homemade costumes and compete for recognition among their peers.

Games were a major part of school Halloween parties in the 1940s. Classic games like bobbing for apples, pin the tail on the donkey, and sack races were popular choices, as they required minimal materials and could be easily organized in the classroom or on the schoolyard. For many children, these simple but fun activities were a highlight of the day, offering a chance to play with friends and enjoy the holiday.

Teachers often read spooky stories to the students, further adding to the Halloween atmosphere. These stories might feature ghosts, witches, or haunted houses, but they were generally mild enough to keep the younger children entertained without being too frightened. Halloween songs and poems were also common, with students learning to sing or recite festive rhymes in celebration of the holiday.

Community Halloween Events and Parades

In addition to school parties, many communities organized Halloween events specifically for children. Local civic groups, churches, and neighborhood associations often hosted Halloween carnivals, parades, or parties where children could gather for an evening of fun. These events were particularly important during the wartime years, as they provided a safe and structured environment for children to celebrate Halloween while also promoting a sense of community.

Halloween parades were a major attraction for children, offering them the chance to march through the streets in their costumes while neighbors cheered them on. Some towns and cities held elaborate parades, complete with floats and live music, while smaller communities organized more modest processions. Regardless of the scale, these parades were a source of pride for children, as they got to showcase their costumes to the entire community.

Community Halloween carnivals often featured games, prizes, and candy, all of which were eagerly anticipated by children. Some carnivals included haunted house attractions, where children could walk through spooky settings filled with fake cobwebs, eerie music, and costumed actors. For many children, visiting a haunted house at the local Halloween carnival was a thrilling part of the holiday, offering just the right amount of scare.

These community events also provided parents with peace of mind, as they knew their children were celebrating Halloween in a safe environment. In an era before widespread trick-or-treating had fully taken hold, organized events like these were a popular way for children to enjoy the holiday without wandering too far from home.

Trick-or-Treating: A Growing Tradition

During the war years, sugar rationing meant that candy was scarce, so children often received homemade treats like popcorn balls, cookies, or apples. In some cases, neighbors would give out small trinkets like buttons, pencils, or crayons instead of candy. Children were usually excited to receive any kind of treat, as the emphasis was on the fun of dressing up and participating in the tradition.

By the late 1940s, as sugar rationing ended and the economy recovered, candy became more readily available, and trick-or-treating began to take on the form we recognize today. Pre-packaged candy from companies like Hershey's, Mars, and Brach's started to appear in trick-or-treat bags, signaling the beginning of the commercialization of Halloween. For children, this shift was exciting, as it meant that they could fill their bags with a variety of sweet treats after a night of trick-or-treating.

Halloween Games and Activities for Children

Games were a central part of Halloween celebrations for children in the 1940s, whether at school, at home, or at community events. Many of these games were based on traditional Halloween activities that had been passed down through generations, adding a sense of continuity and nostalgia to the celebrations.

Bobbing for apples was one of the most popular games of the time. In this game, a large tub of water was filled with apples, and children had to use their mouths (without their hands) to grab an apple floating in the water. This game was not only fun but also tied to old harvest traditions, making it a favorite at Halloween parties.

Other traditional games included snap apple, in which an apple was tied to a string and hung from the ceiling, with children trying to catch it using only their teeth. Pin the tail on the donkey was another classic game, often given a Halloween twist with themes like pinning the hat on the witch or the tail on the black cat.

Fortune-telling games also played a role in children's Halloween activities. These games were mostly lighthearted. They added a mystical element to the holiday. Children might try to tell their fortunes by peeling an apple in one long strip and throwing it over their shoulder, with the peel supposedly forming the initial of their future spouse's name.

The Joy of Simple Treats

For children in the 1940s, Halloween treats were simple but cherished. During the war years, when candy was scarce, homemade treats like caramel apples, popcorn balls, and cookies were often the highlight of the holiday. Many families made their own sweets using rationed ingredients, with recipes that had been passed down through generations.

As sugar became more available in the post-war years, candy slowly returned to Halloween celebrations. Children eagerly anticipated the chance to collect chocolate bars, gumdrops, and other sweet treats during their Halloween activities. By the late 1940s, pre-packaged candy had become more common, and candy companies began to market their products specifically for Halloween, signaling the beginning of a new era in Halloween treats.

The Magic of Halloween for Children in the 1940s

For children growing up in the 1940s, Halloween was a magical time filled with costumes, games, and the excitement of trick-or-treating. Despite the challenges of the war years, children found joy in the simple pleasures of homemade costumes, community events, and creative games. As the decade progressed, Halloween traditions began to evolve, with the post-war economic boom leading to the rise of commercial candy and store-bought costumes. Still, the spirit of Halloween remained rooted in creativity, fun, and the thrill of being a child during one of the most enchanting holidays of the year.

Chapter 11: The Impact of Advertising on Halloween

The 1940s were a transitional time for Halloween, as the holiday evolved from a relatively modest celebration into a more commercialized and widely marketed event. Halloween was not as heavily influenced by advertising in the early years of the decade due to World War II and the economic limitations imposed by rationing. The post-war boom in consumerism saw businesses increasingly capitalize on the holiday. The rise of mass media, combined with the growing influence of advertising in American culture, had a profound effect on how Halloween was celebrated, turning it into an event that companies eagerly sought to exploit.

This chapter explores how advertising began to shape Halloween in the 1940s, with a particular focus on how candy, costumes, and decorations became integral to the holiday's commercial appeal.

Early Wartime Advertising: Subdued and Practical

During the early 1940s, the effects of World War II limited the extent to which Halloween could be commercialized. With widespread rationing and economic challenges, companies were unable to promote luxury goods or indulge in extravagant holiday marketing campaigns. Instead, advertising during this period was often subdued and practical, with a focus on encouraging Americans to conserve resources and support the war effort. Candy and costume advertisements were relatively rare, and when they did appear, they often promoted homemade alternatives or inexpensive solutions.

Many wartime advertisements urged Americans to make do with what they had. For example, instead of promoting new Halloween costumes, advertisers might suggest creative ways to repurpose old clothing or household items into costumes. Magazines and newspapers ran articles with tips on how to turn everyday objects into spooky attire, often accompanied by simple illustrations to inspire families. These advertisements reflected the resourcefulness of the time, emphasizing that Halloween could still be celebrated even in the face of material shortages.

The same was true for candy, which was in short supply due to sugar rationing. Candy companies like Hershey's and Mars, while still producing their products, could not launch large-scale Halloween marketing campaigns due to limited production capabilities. Instead, companies often focused on promoting the importance of rationing and supporting the troops, with the implicit message that their products would be available in greater quantities once the war ended. Homemade treats were encouraged as an alternative, and many advertisements for baking ingredients or household items offered recipes for Halloween cookies, popcorn balls, and caramel apples.

Post-War Boom: The Rise of Consumerism and Advertising

When World War II ended in 1945, American life began to shift dramatically. The post-war economic boom brought a surge of consumerism, with businesses eager to meet the growing demand for goods that had been restricted during the war years. The advertising industry experienced significant growth during this period, as companies sought to capitalize on the newfound prosperity and the expanding middle class. Halloween, like other holidays, became a prime target for advertisers looking to promote their products.

One of the most noticeable changes in post-war Halloween advertising was the increased focus on candy. With sugar rationing lifted and candy production ramping up, companies like Hershey's, Mars, and Brach's began to advertise their products specifically for Halloween. For the first time, candy was marketed as an essential part of the holiday, with advertisements encouraging parents to buy bags of individually wrapped sweets to hand out to trick-or-treaters.

These advertisements often depicted happy, costumed children going door-to-door with bags or baskets, eagerly collecting candy from generous neighbors. The focus was on fun, convenience, and abundance—themes that resonated with the post-war American consumer. Popular candy bars like Hershey's Milk Chocolate, Baby Ruth, and Tootsie Rolls were prominently featured in advertisements, and the idea of giving out pre-packaged candy as a Halloween treat became more widespread.

This period also saw the introduction of the now-famous "fun size" candy bars, which were smaller versions of regular candy bars, packaged specifically for trick-or-treating. Candy companies embraced the idea of making their products more accessible and convenient for the holiday, reinforcing the link between Halloween and candy consumption.

The Commercialization of Costumes and Decorations

In addition to candy, Halloween costumes and decorations became increasingly commercialized in the late 1940s. Companies like Ben Cooper and Collegeville began mass-producing Halloween costumes, which were sold in department stores and five-and-dime stores across the country. These costumes, often made of inexpensive materials like rayon or plastic, allowed children to dress as popular characters from movies, comic books, and radio shows.

Advertising for these costumes emphasized their affordability and ease of use. Parents were encouraged to purchase ready-made costumes rather than spending time and effort creating homemade versions. Popular characters like *Superman*, *Captain Marvel*, *Frankenstein's Monster*, and *The Lone Ranger* appeared in costume advertisements, appealing to children's desire to emulate their favorite heroes and monsters. These costumes often came with simple masks made of plastic or fabric, completing the look and allowing children to fully immerse themselves in the characters they admired.

Halloween decorations also became more commercialized during this period, with companies like Beistle producing a wide range of paper decorations for the holiday. Advertisements for these decorations appeared in magazines, encouraging families to purchase garlands, cutouts, and other items to transform their homes into spooky settings for Halloween. These decorations were inexpensive and easy to use, making them appealing to the growing middle class, who now had more disposable income to spend on holiday festivities.

In post-war America, the message was clear: Halloween was not just a night for trick-or-treating; it was an opportunity to celebrate in style with store-bought costumes, candy, and decorations. Advertisers capitalized on the growing enthusiasm for the holiday, positioning their products as essential components of the Halloween experience.

The Influence of Print Media and Radio Advertising

Print media played a crucial role in promoting Halloween during the 1940s, particularly in the post-war years. Magazines and newspapers were filled with Halloween-themed advertisements, offering everything from candy and costumes to party supplies and decorations. Women's magazines like *Good Housekeeping* and *Ladies' Home Journal* often featured full-page ads promoting candy brands or costume manufacturers, alongside articles offering tips on how to host the perfect Halloween party or make festive treats for the children.

Radio, too, was an important medium for Halloween advertising during this time. With millions of Americans tuning in to radio shows every evening, advertisers took advantage of the captive audience to promote Halloween products. Candy companies sponsored Halloween-themed episodes of popular radio programs, with characters mentioning specific brands or offering tips on how to enjoy the holiday. For example, radio hosts might encourage listeners to stock up on candy for trick-or-treaters or suggest ways to decorate the house using the latest Halloween products.

These advertisements not only promoted specific products but also helped shape the narrative of Halloween as a fun, family-friendly holiday centered around consumer goods. By the end of the 1940s, Halloween had become a major marketing opportunity, with advertisers recognizing the potential to turn the holiday into a profitable event.

Advertising and the Shift in Halloween Traditions

The increased influence of advertising during the 1940s led to a shift in how Halloween was celebrated. As candy, costumes, and decorations became more readily available and affordable, families began to rely more on store-bought items, moving away from the homemade traditions that had once defined Halloween.

This shift was driven in part by the broader trends of post-war consumerism. After years of wartime scarcity, Americans were eager to embrace the convenience and abundance of mass-produced goods. Advertising reinforced the idea that buying candy, costumes, and decorations was not only easier but also more enjoyable. The holiday was increasingly framed as an opportunity to indulge, celebrate, and make memories with the help of store-bought products.

By the end of the 1940s, Halloween had become a more commercialized event, laying the groundwork for the even more consumer-driven holiday that would emerge in the following decades. Advertising played a key role in this transformation, helping to turn Halloween into a major marketing event and solidifying its place in the American commercial calendar.

Conclusion: The Legacy of 1940s Halloween Advertising

The 1940s marked a turning point in the commercialization of Halloween, as advertising began to play a more prominent role in shaping how the holiday was celebrated. From candy and costumes to decorations and party supplies, advertisers recognized the potential of Halloween as a marketing opportunity and worked to promote their products as essential components of the holiday experience.

The early years of the decade were marked by wartime limitations, but the post-war economic boom saw a surge in Halloween advertising, with companies eager to capitalize on the growing consumer market. The legacy of 1940s Halloween advertising can still be seen today, as the holiday continues to be one of the most heavily marketed events of the year. What began as a modest, homemade celebration gradually evolved into the commercial extravaganza we now associate with Halloween, driven in large part by the influence of advertising.

Chapter 12: Ghost Stories and Folklore

Ghost stories and folklore have been at the heart of Halloween celebrations for centuries. In the 1940s, these traditions remained strong, providing thrills and chills for children and adults alike. The holiday had begun to take on more commercial aspects during this decade. The storytelling traditions of Halloween retained their powerful grip on the imaginations of those who celebrated it. Ghost stories, urban legends, and local folklore helped create the spooky atmosphere that made Halloween so exciting. This chapter explores the ghost stories and folklore that shaped Halloween in the 1940s and how these tales contributed to the magic and mystery of the holiday.

The Importance of Storytelling in 1940s Halloween Celebrations

Before the age of television, storytelling played a central role in Halloween festivities. Families and friends would gather around fires, candles, or dimly lit rooms to share spooky tales, evoking images of haunted houses, restless spirits, and mysterious creatures lurking in the dark. This tradition, which has roots in ancient harvest festivals, became an essential part of Halloween during the 1940s.

For many families, ghost stories were a way to bring the supernatural and the unknown into the home in a safe, controlled manner. In an era when much of life was dictated by war and hardship, ghost stories offered an escape into the world of fantasy and fear. These stories were not only entertaining, but they also provided a way to explore themes of death, the afterlife, and the unknown, all of which resonated with a society that had recently endured the horrors of World War II.

During Halloween, ghost stories were often told as part of a larger celebration. After an evening of trick-or-treating or a community party, children would gather around with their parents or friends to hear spine-chilling tales. These stories, passed down from older generations or pulled from local folklore, served as a rite of passage for young listeners, who delighted in the thrill of being scared while knowing they were still safe at home.

Classic Ghost Stories of the 1940s

Many of the ghost stories told during Halloween in the 1940s had been passed down through generations. These stories often featured familiar settings—haunted houses, dark forests, or desolate graveyards—where restless spirits wandered in search of revenge, redemption, or resolution. Some of the most popular ghost stories of the time included classic tales that had been adapted or reimagined for new audiences.

One of the most enduring ghost stories told during this period was *The Legend of Sleepy Hollow* by Washington Irving. This early American tale, set in the quiet village of Sleepy Hollow, follows the hapless schoolteacher Ichabod Crane as he encounters the terrifying Headless Horseman, a ghostly figure said to haunt the area. The story's mix of suspense, humor, and supernatural elements made it a perfect fit for Halloween, and it was a favorite of children and adults alike. Many families would read or tell *The Legend of Sleepy Hollow* as part of their Halloween tradition, bringing the mysterious world of Sleepy Hollow into their homes.

Another popular ghost story was *The Monkey's Paw* by W.W. Jacobs. This short story, first published in 1902, tells the tale of a family who comes into possession of a magical monkey's paw that grants three wishes—each with tragic, unintended consequences. The eerie tone and moral lesson of the story made it a favorite for Halloween, with its theme of be careful what you wish for resonating strongly with listeners.

Edgar Allan Poe's work also found a place in Halloween storytelling during the 1940s. Stories like *The Tell-Tale Heart* and *The Raven* were frequently recited or dramatized during Halloween celebrations. Poe's mastery of suspense and psychological horror made his stories ideal for creating a chilling atmosphere, and his work was well known to both children and adults. Reciting *The Raven* or reading *The Tell-Tale Heart* by candlelight was a popular activity at Halloween parties, especially among teenagers and young adults seeking a more intense scare.

Local Folklore and Urban Legends

In addition to these classic ghost stories, local folklore and urban legends played a significant role in shaping Halloween storytelling during the 1940s. Every town or region seemed to have its own haunted house, ghostly figure, or mysterious event that had been passed down through generations. These local legends were often told with a mix of sincerity and humor, with each storyteller adding their own embellishments to make the tale even more frightening.

For example, many rural communities had stories about haunted farms or abandoned buildings where ghosts or strange creatures were said to roam. These stories often took the form of cautionary tales, warning children not to wander too far from home or venture into certain areas after dark. In some cases, these legends were based on real events—a tragic death, a mysterious disappearance, or a long-forgotten crime—that had been exaggerated over time to become part of local lore.

One common urban legend that circulated during this time was the tale of the hitchhiking ghost. In this story, a driver picks up a young woman or man who appears to be stranded on the side of the road. After giving the hitchhiker a ride, the driver arrives at their destination, only to find that the hitchhiker has disappeared—revealing that they were a ghost all along. This story, in its various forms, was told across the country, often with the setting and details adjusted to fit the local area.

Urban legends like these added an element of local color to Halloween storytelling, making the tales feel more personal and immediate. For children and teenagers, these stories were particularly exciting, as they often involved familiar places and people, making the supernatural seem all the more real.

Folklore Rooted in Harvest Traditions

Much of the folklore surrounding Halloween in the 1940s was rooted in older traditions that dated back to harvest festivals and pagan rituals. These traditions, which celebrated the end of the harvest season and the approach of winter, often included elements of superstition and magic. Halloween in the 1940s, like the Halloweens before it, was a time when the veil between the living and the dead was said to be at its thinnest, making it an ideal night for ghostly encounters and supernatural happenings.

Fortune-telling games, which had been popular for centuries, remained a common activity during Halloween celebrations in the 1940s. Children and teenagers would participate in games designed to predict their futures, particularly in matters of love and marriage. One traditional game involved peeling an apple in one long strip and throwing it over the shoulder—the shape of the peel was said to reveal the first initial of one's future spouse. Another game involved cracking an egg into a glass of water and interpreting the shapes formed by the egg white, with different shapes supposedly indicating different future events.

These fortune-telling games, while lighthearted and fun, were deeply rooted in the ancient belief that Halloween was a time when the future could be glimpsed, and the supernatural world was closer to our own. They added a sense of mystery and excitement to Halloween, encouraging participants to think about the unknown and what the future might hold.

Ghost Stories in Popular Media

Radio shows and movies in the 1940s played a significant role in bringing ghost stories and folklore to wider audiences. As discussed in previous chapters, radio programs like *Lights Out* and *Suspense* aired special Halloween episodes that featured ghost stories and eerie tales. These programs were hugely popular, with families gathering around the radio to listen to the latest spooky broadcast. The power of sound in these radio dramas helped bring ghost stories to life in vivid and terrifying ways, making them an essential part of Halloween for many listeners.

Movies, too, capitalized on the appeal of ghost stories and folklore. Hollywood produced numerous films in the 1940s that featured haunted houses, restless spirits, and other supernatural elements. Films like *The Uninvited* (1944), which tells the story of a brother and sister who move into a house haunted by a tragic past, reflected the growing interest in ghost stories on the big screen. These films, while often mild by today's horror standards, provided plenty of frights and fed into the public's fascination with the supernatural.

Conclusion: The Enduring Power of Ghost Stories and Folklore

Ghost stories and folklore were an essential part of Halloween in the 1940s, providing entertainment, thrills, and a connection to older traditions. Whether told by the fireside, on the radio, or through the magic of cinema, these stories captured the imagination of children and adults alike. The combination of local legends, classic ghost tales, and ancient superstitions created a rich tapestry of storytelling that made Halloween one of the most exciting times of the year. Even as Halloween became more commercialized in the post-war years, the tradition of sharing ghost stories remained a central part of the holiday, keeping alive the mystery and magic that has always defined Halloween.

Chapter 13: Halloween in Small Towns vs. Cities

Halloween in the 1940s, much like today, was celebrated differently depending on where one lived. The experience of Halloween in small towns contrasted with that of Halloween in cities, with each setting offering its own unique traditions, activities, and challenges. In small towns, the holiday often had a more intimate, community-focused atmosphere, while city dwellers experienced Halloween on a larger, more bustling scale. This chapter explores the differences in how Halloween was celebrated in small towns versus urban areas during the 1940s, highlighting the role of community, safety, and local culture in shaping the holiday experience.

Halloween in Small Towns: Community and Tradition

In small towns across America, Halloween was a deeply community-centered holiday in the 1940s. With fewer residents and a closer-knit social structure, small towns fostered an environment where nearly everyone knew each other, making Halloween feel like a shared event for the entire town. Neighbors looked out for each other's children, and many families participated in Halloween activities together, creating a sense of unity and safety that was harder to find in larger cities.

One of the hallmarks of Halloween in small towns was the emphasis on homemade traditions. Costumes, decorations, and even treats were often made by hand, reflecting the resourcefulness and creativity of small-town life. In rural areas, where access to store-bought goods might be limited, families relied on what they had at home to celebrate the holiday. Old clothes were repurposed into costumes, and pumpkins from local farms were carved into jack-o'-lanterns. Children in small towns were more likely to receive homemade treats like popcorn balls, cookies, or caramel apples when trick-or-treating, as opposed to the store-bought candy that was becoming more common in urban areas.

Small towns also had their own unique Halloween traditions. In many rural communities, Halloween was closely tied to the harvest season, and activities like hayrides, corn mazes, and bonfires were popular ways to celebrate. These events were often organized by local churches, schools, or civic groups and provided a safe, family-friendly environment for children and adults alike. Halloween carnivals, complete with games, costume contests, and homemade food, were a staple of small-town celebrations. These events allowed the entire community to come together, reinforcing the bonds of friendship and neighborliness.

In terms of trick-or-treating, small towns offered a much more manageable and familiar experience than cities. Children would often go door-to-door in their immediate neighborhoods, visiting houses of people they knew personally. This created a strong sense of security, as parents trusted their neighbors and knew that their children would be safe while trick-or-treating. The relatively small size of these towns meant that children could cover most of the town on foot, collecting treats from friends, family members, and familiar faces.

Halloween in Cities: Crowds, Excitement, and Urban Challenges

In contrast to the close-knit celebrations of small towns, Halloween in cities during the 1940s was a larger, more bustling affair. Urban areas offered a wider range of activities, but they also presented unique challenges, particularly in terms of safety and logistics. Cities were home to more people, more businesses, and more traffic, which meant that Halloween required a greater level of organization and supervision to ensure that children could celebrate safely.

One of the key differences between urban and small-town Halloweens was the scale of trick-or-treating. In cities, children could visit dozens or even hundreds of homes in a single night, especially in densely populated neighborhoods where houses or apartment buildings were packed closely together. This made the trick-or-treating experience in cities both exciting and overwhelming, as children had access to a greater variety of treats and decorations, but also had to navigate larger crowds and more complicated streets.

City trick-or-treaters were often rewarded with store-bought candy, as urban residents were more likely to purchase treats from local stores than to make homemade ones. This shift toward commercialized candy was a sign of the growing consumer culture in post-war America, particularly in cities where stores were more accessible and mass-produced goods were more widely available. Advertisements for candy brands like Hershey's, Tootsie Rolls, and Mars bars appeared frequently in urban newspapers and magazines, encouraging city dwellers to stock up on treats for Halloween.

Halloween parades were a common feature in cities, drawing crowds of families and spectators who came to see children march in their costumes or ride on elaborately decorated floats. These parades were often sponsored by local businesses or civic organizations, with prizes awarded for the best costumes or floats. City parks and recreation departments also organized Halloween carnivals and parties, offering games, food, and entertainment for children and their families.

However, the sheer size and complexity of cities presented challenges for Halloween safety. With more traffic on the streets and larger crowds of people, parents in cities often had to take extra precautions when sending their children out to trick-or-treat. In some cases, parents would form groups and accompany their children, ensuring that they stayed safe in the busy urban environment. In densely populated areas, children might visit apartment buildings instead of individual houses, which presented a different set of challenges, such as gaining access to secured buildings or navigating busy stairwells and elevators.

Community and Neighborhood Bonds

Despite the differences in scale and setting, both small-town and city Halloweens relied heavily on a sense of community. In small towns, the holiday fostered close ties between neighbors, who often knew each other personally and worked together to create a safe, festive environment for children. Community events like carnivals, parades, and bonfires helped reinforce these bonds, providing a space for families to celebrate together.

In cities, where residents might not know all of their neighbors personally, Halloween still provided an opportunity to foster a sense of community. Apartment buildings, neighborhoods, and local businesses often organized their own Halloween events, allowing urban dwellers to come together and celebrate the holiday in a safe and controlled setting. In some cases, entire city blocks would be decorated for Halloween, with residents going all out to create elaborate displays that drew visitors from across the city. These block-wide efforts helped to create a sense of neighborhood pride and cohesion, even in the bustling, anonymous environment of the city.

The shared experience of Halloween, whether in a small town or a big city, brought people together. The holiday served as a reminder that, despite the differences in lifestyle between rural and urban America, there were certain traditions and celebrations that united the country. Children in both settings eagerly looked forward to Halloween each year, donning costumes, playing games, and indulging in treats, regardless of where they lived.

Halloween Safety in Small Towns and Cities

Safety was a key concern for parents and community leaders in both small towns and cities, particularly during the 1940s, when the war and its aftermath created new challenges. In small towns, safety was often maintained through personal relationships and community involvement. Neighbors kept an eye out for each other's children, and older siblings often accompanied younger children while trick-or-treating. Small towns also had fewer cars on the road, which reduced the risk of traffic accidents during Halloween night.

In cities, however, safety required more formal measures. Police departments often increased patrols on Halloween to ensure that children could trick-or-treat without fear of getting lost or encountering dangerous situations. Some neighborhoods established trick-or-treating hours to limit the time children were out on the streets, and parents were encouraged to inspect their children's candy to make sure it was safe to eat. Urban schools and community organizations also emphasized the importance of Halloween safety, teaching children how to navigate city streets and avoid potential dangers.

Despite these precautions, Halloween remained a time of fun and excitement in both small towns and cities. Whether they were celebrating in the familiar, intimate setting of a small town or the fast-paced, crowded environment of a city, children eagerly embraced the spirit of the holiday, enjoying the chance to dress up, collect treats, and participate in the spooky festivities.

The Role of Tradition and Local Culture

Local culture played a significant role in shaping how Halloween was celebrated in both small towns and cities. In rural areas, where farming and agriculture were central to life, Halloween often took on a harvest festival theme. Hayrides, corn mazes, and apple bobbing were popular activities that reflected the agricultural roots of the community. In cities, where cultural diversity was more pronounced, Halloween celebrations often incorporated traditions from various immigrant communities, adding new elements to the holiday.

For example, in cities with large Irish or Scottish populations, Halloween traditions like carving turnips (an early precursor to the jack-o'-lantern) or telling ghost stories with Celtic origins might be incorporated into local celebrations. In neighborhoods with large Hispanic populations, traditions like *Dia de los Muertos* (Day of the

Dead) sometimes blended with Halloween, adding a layer of cultural richness to the holiday.

These local traditions and cultural influences helped make Halloween unique in each town or city, offering a glimpse into the diverse ways in which Americans celebrated the holiday.

Conclusion: The Unique Spirit of Halloween in Small Towns and Cities

Halloween in the 1940s offered a fascinating glimpse into the diversity of American life. In small towns, the holiday was an intimate, community-driven event, where neighbors came together to celebrate with homemade treats, costumes, and traditional harvest-themed activities. In cities, Halloween was a larger, more bustling affair, with big parades, commercialized candy, and a wider variety of activities for children to enjoy.

Despite these differences, the essence of Halloween—fun, creativity, and community—remained the same. Whether celebrated in the heart of a small town or the bustling streets of a big city, Halloween in the 1940s was a night filled with magic and excitement, offering children and families the chance to come together and celebrate the spooky, mysterious, and joyful aspects of the holiday.

Chapter 14: The Role of Schools and Churches in Halloween Celebrations

Schools and churches played a pivotal role in Halloween celebrations during the 1940s. At a time when communities were tightly knit, especially during the war years, these institutions served as hubs for social gatherings and events, including those related to holidays like Halloween. For children, schools were often the centerpiece of their Halloween fun. Churches also provided a safe and controlled environment for families to celebrate. This chapter explores how schools and churches contributed to Halloween in the 1940s, providing spaces for parties, games, and traditions that reflected the values of the time.

Schools as Halloween Centers

During the 1940s, schools were the primary setting for many children's Halloween celebrations. With trick-or-treating not yet the dominant Halloween activity it would become in later decades, school-organized events filled an essential role in providing a safe and structured environment for Halloween fun. Teachers and administrators took great care in transforming classrooms and auditoriums into festive spaces, fostering excitement for the holiday.

Classroom Decorations and Activities

In the weeks leading up to Halloween, classrooms were often filled with decorations that reflected the spooky spirit of the season. Students, with guidance from their teachers, made paper jack-o'-lanterns, black cats, witches, and skeletons, which adorned the walls of classrooms and hallways. These crafts were not only fun for students but also served as a way to teach lessons on art and creativity, with children learning how to cut out intricate shapes or paint detailed Halloween-themed scenes.

On Halloween day itself, many schools hosted special celebrations during the school day. Children arrived at school dressed in their costumes, excited to show off their homemade or store-bought outfits to classmates and teachers. Some schools organized costume parades, where students marched through the hallways or gathered in the schoolyard to display their costumes for the rest of the school to see. These parades often included costume contests, with prizes awarded for the scariest, funniest, or most creative costumes. Teachers and parents might serve as judges, adding an element of friendly competition to the festivities.

Halloween Games and Traditions

In addition to costume parades, schools organized a variety of games and activities for Halloween. Games like bobbing for apples, pin the hat on the witch, and sack races were popular choices for Halloween parties. These games were easy to set up and required minimal materials, making them perfect for classrooms or schoolyards. For students, these games provided a chance to burn off energy and enjoy some friendly competition with their peers.

Storytelling was another important aspect of school Halloween celebrations. Teachers might read ghost stories or recite Halloween-themed poems to their students, creating an eerie yet fun atmosphere in the classroom. In some schools, older students took on the role of storytellers, sharing spooky tales with the younger children in dimly lit rooms, with the lights turned low to enhance the mood.

Tales of haunted houses, witches, and ghosts became an integral part of Halloween celebrations at school, helping to reinforce the themes of mystery and the supernatural that defined the holiday.

Halloween Parties and Events

Beyond the classroom, schools often hosted Halloween parties in the evening, providing students and their families with a place to celebrate after the school day had ended. These parties were highly anticipated events, featuring a mix of games, music, and food. School gyms or auditoriums were transformed into spooky settings, with decorations like paper skeletons, orange and black streamers, and pumpkin centerpieces. Teachers, parents, and local community leaders often volunteered to organize these events, ensuring that the entire school community could come together for the occasion.

Food was an important part of these parties, though wartime rationing sometimes limited what could be served. Popcorn balls, homemade cookies, and caramel apples were common treats at school Halloween parties, offering children a sweet reward after a day of fun. In some cases, parents contributed to the party by bringing in homemade baked goods or simple snacks, adding a communal aspect to the event.

These school Halloween parties helped reinforce a sense of community, providing a space where children could enjoy the holiday in a safe and supervised environment. They also reflected the values of the 1940s, emphasizing togetherness, creativity, and resourcefulness in the face of challenges like rationing.

Churches and Halloween: Safe Havens for Families

Churches played an equally important role in Halloween celebrations during the 1940s. For many families, particularly those in rural areas or small towns, the local church was the center of social life, hosting community events and gatherings throughout the year. Halloween was no exception, and churches often organized events that offered a wholesome, family-friendly alternative to more rowdy celebrations.

Church-Sponsored Halloween Parties

Church-sponsored Halloween parties were common in the 1940s, especially in communities where trick-or-treating had not yet become the norm. These parties were designed to provide a safe environment for children and their families to enjoy the holiday, free from the pranks and mischief that sometimes accompanied Halloween in less supervised settings.

At these parties, families could participate in many of the same activities found at school events, including costume contests, games, and storytelling. However, church-sponsored parties often had a more subdued and respectful tone, reflecting the values of the congregation.

Costumes were still encouraged, but parents were often mindful to ensure that their children's outfits were in line with the church's expectations—avoiding anything too gory or frightening.

In some cases, churches hosted community-wide Halloween carnivals, complete with booths offering games, food, and entertainment. These carnivals were a major event in many small towns, drawing families from the surrounding area. Games like ring toss, apple bobbing, and fishing for prizes were popular attractions, providing children with a fun, interactive way to celebrate Halloween in a wholesome environment.

Fortune-Telling and Games with a Twist

One unique aspect of church-sponsored Halloween events in the 1940s was the inclusion of fortune-telling games and activities that were designed to be lighthearted rather than occult in nature. Traditional Halloween fortune-telling games, such as interpreting apple peels or reading egg whites, had roots in older folk customs. Churches often adapted these activities to align with their teachings.

For example, instead of using traditional fortune-telling methods, church Halloween events might feature games where children pulled slips of paper from a cauldron, each with a humorous or encouraging message about their future. This allowed families to participate in the playful aspects of fortune-telling without straying too far from the church's values. These games maintained the fun and mystery of Halloween while ensuring that the activities remained appropriate for all members of the congregation.

The Role of Harvest Festivals

In addition to Halloween-specific events, many churches in the 1940s held harvest festivals around the same time of year. These festivals, which celebrated the bounty of the autumn harvest, often took place in October and featured many of the same activities associated with Halloween, such as hayrides, bonfires, and pumpkin carving.

For some churches, the harvest festival served as an alternative to Halloween, focusing on themes of gratitude and community rather than the supernatural or spooky. Families would gather for an evening of food, games, and fellowship, with the church providing a safe and welcoming space for the celebration. These harvest festivals were distinct from Halloween, but they often overlapped in terms of timing and activities, contributing to the overall festive atmosphere of the season.

Balancing Fun and Morality

One of the key challenges for churches in the 1940s was balancing the fun and excitement of Halloween with the moral and religious values of the congregation. Halloween had long been associated with themes of death, ghosts, and the supernatural. However, many churches sought to downplay these aspects of the holiday in favor of more wholesome activities.

At church-sponsored Halloween events, the emphasis was often placed on creativity, community, and family-friendly fun, with less focus on the darker, more macabre elements of the holiday. This approach allowed churches to engage with the holiday in a way that aligned with their teachings while still providing children with a chance to participate in the excitement of Halloween.

Conclusion: Schools and Churches as Pillars of Halloween Celebrations

In the 1940s, schools and churches played a central role in shaping how Halloween was celebrated. These institutions provided children and their families with safe, structured environments where they could enjoy the holiday without the worries of mischief or danger. From costume parades and games in the classroom to church-sponsored parties and harvest festivals, schools and churches helped create a sense of community around Halloween, reinforcing the values of togetherness, creativity, and fun.

As Halloween continued to evolve in the post-war years, schools and churches remained important venues for Halloween celebrations, ensuring that the holiday retained its place as a cherished event for children and families alike.

Chapter 15: Halloween and the Changing Face of America

The 1940s were a transformative decade for the United States. With the challenges of World War II and the economic recovery that followed, the nation saw profound changes in its social, cultural, and economic landscape. Halloween, like many aspects of American life, reflected these shifts. As the decade progressed, the holiday evolved from a modest, community-centered celebration into a more commercialized event, setting the stage for the Halloween we recognize today. This chapter explores how Halloween in the 1940s both mirrored and influenced the broader changes in American society and how these transformations laid the groundwork for the future of the holiday.

The Impact of World War II on American Life and Halloween

World War II, which dominated much of the early 1940s, had a significant impact on Halloween and on American life in general. The war affected nearly every facet of daily life, from food and clothing to entertainment and social gatherings. Rationing, a defining feature of wartime America, meant that many traditional Halloween items—such as candy, costumes, and decorations—were either scarce or unavailable.

The limitations imposed by the war led to a more resourceful approach to Halloween celebrations. Families made their own costumes from available materials, relying on creativity and ingenuity rather than store-bought goods. Homemade treats replaced store-bought candy, with families preparing popcorn balls, caramel apples, and cookies instead of the chocolate bars and sweets that would dominate post-war Halloweens. Decorations, too, were often homemade, with simple paper cutouts, jack-o'-lanterns, and other do-it-yourself projects transforming homes for the holiday.

Despite these limitations, Halloween during the war years took on a deeper meaning for many families. The holiday provided a welcome escape from the hardships of daily life, offering children and adults alike a brief respite from the anxieties of war. Community events, such as school and church-sponsored Halloween parties, became even more important, serving as spaces where families could gather to celebrate in a safe and supportive environment.

As American soldiers fought overseas, Halloween also became a way to boost morale on the home front. Patriotic themes were often incorporated into Halloween costumes and decorations, with children dressing as soldiers, sailors, or nurses. These costumes reflected the national mood of solidarity and support for the war effort, reinforcing the idea that everyone, including children, had a role to play in helping the country succeed.

Post-War Prosperity and the Commercialization of Halloween

The end of World War II in 1945 ushered in a new era of prosperity for the United States. The post-war economic boom, often referred to as the "Golden Age of Capitalism," saw rising incomes, increased consumerism, and the expansion of the American middle class. This period of economic growth had a profound effect on holidays like Halloween, as the country shifted from the austerity of wartime to a culture of abundance and consumption.

One of the most significant changes to Halloween in the post-war years was the rise of commercialism. As rationing ended and consumer goods became more readily available, businesses quickly recognized the marketing potential of Halloween. Candy companies, costume manufacturers, and decoration producers began to target Halloween specifically, turning the holiday into a major sales opportunity.

Candy, in particular, became a central part of Halloween celebrations in the late 1940s. With sugar rationing lifted, candy manufacturers ramped up production, and candy advertisements appeared in magazines, newspapers, and on the radio. Pre-packaged candy bars, such as Hershey's and Baby Ruth, were marketed as the perfect treats for trick-or-treaters, encouraging families to buy bags of candy to hand out on Halloween night.

Costumes, too, became increasingly commercialized. Companies like Ben Cooper and Collegeville produced affordable, ready-made Halloween costumes for children, featuring popular characters from movies, radio shows, and comic books. These mass-produced costumes allowed children to easily dress up as their favorite heroes or monsters, reducing the need for homemade costumes. Costumes featuring characters like Superman, Captain Marvel, and Frankenstein's monster became staples of Halloween, reflecting the growing influence of mass media on the holiday.

Halloween decorations also became more elaborate and widely available. Companies like Beistle produced paper decorations, including garlands, cutouts, and posters, that could be purchased at local stores. These decorations, often featuring classic Halloween imagery like witches, bats, skeletons, and jack-o'-lanterns, helped families create a festive atmosphere in their homes with minimal effort.

The commercialization of Halloween during the post-war years was part of a broader trend in American society. As the economy grew and consumer goods became more accessible, holidays like Halloween became opportunities for businesses to market their products and for families to indulge in the pleasures of consumption. This shift marked the beginning of Halloween's transformation into the heavily commercialized event we recognize today.

The Influence of Mass Media on Halloween

The rise of mass media in the 1940s played a significant role in shaping how Halloween was celebrated. Movies, radio, and, toward the end of the decade, television, all contributed to the growing popularity of Halloween and influenced the costumes, themes, and activities associated with the holiday.

Horror films, in particular, left a lasting mark on Halloween. The 1940s saw the release of several iconic horror films from Universal

Pictures, including *The Wolf Man* (1941) and *Frankenstein Meets the Wolf Man* (1943). These films, featuring classic monsters like Frankenstein's monster, Dracula, and the Wolf Man, became closely associated with Halloween, inspiring costumes and party themes across the country.

Radio, still the dominant form of entertainment during much of the 1940s, also played a key role in Halloween celebrations. Popular radio shows like *Lights Out* and *Suspense* aired special Halloween episodes that featured ghost stories, supernatural events, and eerie sound effects. Families would gather around the radio on Halloween night to listen to these broadcasts, creating a shared experience that added to the holiday's spooky atmosphere.

As television began to make its way into American homes in the late 1940s, it too influenced Halloween traditions. Television shows started to incorporate Halloween-themed episodes, bringing the holiday into living rooms in a new and exciting way. Although television's influence on Halloween would become more pronounced in the 1950s and beyond, its early presence in the 1940s helped to solidify Halloween's place in American popular culture.

The Evolving Role of Community

Schools, churches, and local civic groups continued to play a central role in organizing Halloween events, providing children and families with safe and structured spaces to celebrate.

In small towns, Halloween was often a community-wide affair, with neighbors coming together to host parties, carnivals, and parades. Trick-or-treating, while growing in popularity, was still largely a neighborhood activity, with children visiting the homes of people they knew personally. This sense of familiarity and safety was a defining feature of small-town Halloween celebrations, reinforcing the idea that Halloween was a time for families and communities to come together.

In larger cities, Halloween took on a more bustling and diverse character. Urban neighborhoods, with their dense populations and busy streets, provided children with more opportunities for trick-or-treating, and citywide parades and events offered a wider range of activities. However, the sheer size of cities also presented challenges, particularly in terms of safety. Police departments and community leaders worked to ensure that Halloween remained a fun and safe holiday for city children, often organizing events like costume contests, haunted houses, and parties in local parks or community centers.

Despite the differences between small-town and urban Halloween celebrations, the holiday's core themes of fun, creativity, and community remained constant. Whether in a small town or a big city, Halloween provided children and families with an opportunity to come together, enjoy each other's company, and indulge in the spooky thrills of the season.

The Legacy of 1940s Halloween: Setting the Stage for the Future

By the end of the 1940s, Halloween had begun to take on the modern characteristics we associate with the holiday today. The commercialization of candy, costumes, and decorations, coupled with the influence of mass media, transformed Halloween into a larger, more widespread event. At the same time, the community-focused traditions of school parties, church events, and neighborhood trick-or-treating ensured that Halloween remained a family-friendly holiday, grounded in the values of creativity, fun, and togetherness.

The changes that occurred in Halloween during the 1940s set the stage for the holiday's continued evolution in the decades to come. As the United States entered the 1950s, Halloween would become even more commercialized, with the rise of television, mass marketing, and the baby boom contributing to the holiday's growth. However, the traditions and values established in the 1940s would remain an enduring part of Halloween, providing a foundation for the holiday's future development.

Conclusion: Halloween as a Reflection of a Changing America

The story of Halloween in the 1940s is, in many ways, a reflection of the broader changes taking place in America during this transformative decade. From the resourcefulness and community spirit of the war years to the prosperity and consumerism of the post-war period, Halloween mirrored the shifts in American society and culture. As the country changed, so too did the holiday, evolving from a modest, homegrown celebration into a commercial and cultural event that would continue to grow in importance and popularity.

By the end of the 1940s, Halloween had become a defining part of American life, offering children and families the chance to celebrate in ways that were both fun and meaningful. The legacy of 1940s Halloween is still evident today, as the traditions and innovations of this decade continue to shape the way we celebrate the holiday in the modern era.